Thomas Patrick Hughes

Notes on Muhammadanism

Being Outlines of the Religious System of Islam

Thomas Patrick Hughes

Notes on Muhammadanism
Being Outlines of the Religious System of Islam

ISBN/EAN: 9783744725644

Printed in Europe, USA, Canada, Australia, Japan

Cover: Foto ©Lupo / pixelio.de

More available books at **www.hansebooks.com**

NOTES

ON

MUHAMMADANISM,

BEING OUTLINES OF

THE RELIGIOUS SYSTEM OF ISLAM.

BY THE

REV. T. P. HUGHES, M.R.A.S.,

C.M.S., MISSIONARY TO THE AFGHANS, PESHAWAR.

SECOND EDITION,

REVISED AND ENLARGED.

LONDON:
WM. H. ALLEN & CO., 13, WATERLOO PLACE, S.W.
PUBLISHERS TO THE INDIA OFFICE.

1877.

(All rights reserved.)

PREFACE

TO THE SECOND EDITION.

THE favourable reception which has been accorded to the first edition of these outlines of the Muhammadan system has encouraged me to put forth a revised and enlarged edition. I am glad of the opportunity; for, the first edition contained numerous errors, consequent upon my bringing it out during a short and hurried visit to England, in the summer of 1875. Still, notwithstanding its numerous and manifest short-comings, it has been pronounced, by an eminent Arabic scholar, as not only "about the best outlines of Muslim faith he had seen"; but as having "*the rare merit of being accurate.*"

T. P. H.

Peshawar, 16th August 1877.

PREFACE

TO THE FIRST EDITION.

THERE is a general impression amongst European students of Islám, that it is a simple system of Deism unfettered by numerous dogmas and creeds, which are supposed to be such an insuperable hindrance to an acceptance of Christianity. Such was the opinion of the historian Gibbon, and it is also the view taken by some who seek to weaken the authority of the Christian system by extolling the merit of its great rival creed. But even amongst the advocates of Christianity there is altogether an erroneous impression as to what Muhammadanism really is. Dean Stanley has an admirable chapter on the subject of Islám in his

"Eastern Church"; but he tells his readers that "*the Qurán contains the whole of the religion of Muhammad*"; and Mr. Zincke, in his exceedingly interesting book, "Egypt of the Pharaohs and the Khedive," appears to be under the same impression; for he says, "*the Qurán is an all embracing and sufficient code, regulating everything.*" Whereas the true state of the case is, that whilst the Qurán is the highest authority for Muslim doctrine, still, the "faithful," whether Sunní, Shía'h, or Wahhábí, must receive the sayings and practices of their Prophet as of divine obligation; for, in Islám, the teachings of the "Sacred Traditions" must be received side by side with that of the Qurán itself; and the Muslim who would escape the suspicion of heresy must not dare to question the teaching of the learned doctors, whose opinions have been handed down in numerous commentaries and ponderous volumes divinity.

In publishing these "Notes on Muhammadanism," the author is fully conscious of their imperfections,* but he ventures to hope that they will contain information which may be suggestive to Missionaries and others interested in the study of Islám.

Upon a thoughtful study of the present work, the reader cannot fail to observe what an important place *dogmatic teaching* occupies in the system under consideration. There are those amongst English and Continental writers who regard all dogmatic teaching as antiquated, and who would recommend the Christian Missionary to keep *dogma* in the back-ground, when dealing with such a religious system as Muhammadanism. But Muslim divines would spurn such teaching as unworthy of theologians, whether of Islám or of Christianity. The trumpet must give no uncertain sound. It is a solemn thing for a Christian Missionary to be engaged day by day in unsettling the

---

* They are *bonâ fide* notes of a Dictionary of Islám, which the author has in course of compilation.

religious opinions of immortal beings, unless he feels that he has something good and true to offer in the place of opinions renounced. If we call upon the millions of Islám to loose from their moorings amidst the reefs and shoals of a false system, and to steer forth into the wide ocean of religious inquiry, we must surely direct them to some fair haven of refuge where they will find rest and peace. It has been well said by Dr. Martensen* that "a mind starved by doubt has never been able to produce a dogmatic system"; and we are quite sure that all who have had practical experience of Muhammadanism, will agree that none could be so helpless in dealing with Muslim doctors, as those who are wandering about in the uncertainty of doubt, and cannot stand firm in the certainty of faith.

On the other hand, Muhammadanism may be used as a schoolmaster to bring men to

---

* "Christian Dogmatics," by Dr. H. Martensen, Bishop of Zeeland, Denmark.

Christ, for much which is contained in its elaborate system is expressive of man's great and exceeding need. The Christian controversialist, in dealing with Muhammadanism, must ever remember that it contains a two-fold element of truth. The Founder of Islám derived much of his system from that great unwritten law of God which is ever speaking to men of every nation and of every clime; and he was also greatly indebted to the written law of the Holy One of Israel, although he received it from Talmudic sources. To quote the words of Bengel, the commentator, "the Law"— whether it be that written on the conscience, or in the pages of the Qurán, or in God's revealed word—"the law hounds a man till he betake himself to Christ; then it says to him, 'Thou hast found an asylum; I pursue thee no more; thou art wise, thou art safe.'"

Notwithstanding its fair show of outward observance, and its severe legal enactments, there is something in Islám which strikes at the very root of morals, poisons domestic life, and (in its truest sense) disorganizes society. Freedom of judgment is crushed, and a barrier has been raised not merely against the advance of Christianity, but against the progress of Civilization itself. It is impossible to account for this peculiar feature in Muhammadan nations by attributing it to the peculiarities of Oriental races, or other accidental circumstances. The great cause lies in the religious system which they profess, which binds them hand and foot. For everything in religion, in law, in life, and in thought, has been measured for all time. Muhammadanism admits of no progress in morals, law, or commerce. It fails to regenerate the man, and it is equally powerless in regenerating the nation.

Putney, 17*th August* 1875.

CONTENTS.

		Page
I.	Muhammad	1
II.	Islam	10
III.	Rule of Faith	12
IV.	The Qurán	14
V.	Inspiration	47
VI.	The Traditions	50
VII.	Ijma'	61
VIII.	Qias	64
IX.	Faith	66
X.	Allah, or God	67
XI.	Angels	79
XII.	Prophets	84
XIII.	The Day of Resurrection and Judgment	87

		Page
XIV.	HEAVEN	91
XV.	HELL	96
XVI.	THE DECREES OF GOD	98
XVII.	THE FIVE FOUNDATIONS OF PRACTICAL RELIGION	101
XVIII.	THE RECITAL OF THE CREED	102
XIX.	PRAYER	104
XX.	RAMAZAN, OR THE MONTH OF FASTING	119
XXI.	ZAKAT, OR LEGAL ALMSGIVING	125
XXII.	HAJJ, OR PILGRIMAGE TO MECCA	130
XXIII.	THE LAW	137
XXIV.	SIN	139
XXV.	PUNISHMENT	141
XXVI.	LAWFUL FOOD	143
XXVII.	FARZ-I-KAFAI	146
XXVIII.	FITRAT	147
XXIX.	SALUTATIONS	148
XXX.	CALIPH	150
XXXI.	MUHAMMADAN CLERGY, SCHOLARS, AND SAINTS	155
XXXII.	THEOLOGICAL LITERATURE	160
XXXIII.	MUHARRAM AND ASHURAA	163

CONTENTS.

		Page
XXXIV.	Akhiri Chahar Shamba . . .	167
XXXV.	Bara Wafat	168
XXXVI.	Shab-i-Barat	169
XXXVII.	'Id-ul-Fitr	171
XXXVIII.	'Id-ul-Azha	173
XXXIX.	Nikah, or Marriage . . .	177
XL.	Talaq, or Divorce	182
XLI.	Janaza, or Burial	185
XLII.	Slavery	194
XLIII.	Khutbah, or the Friday's Sermon .	198
XLIV.	Jihad, or Religious War . . .	206
XLV.	Martyrs	211
XLVI.	The Four Orthodox Sects . .	212
XLVII.	The Shia'hs	214
XLVIII.	The Wahhabis	219
XLIX.	Sufiism, or Mysticism . . .	227
L.	Faqirs, or Darweshes . . .	234
LI.	Zikr, or the Religious Services of the Darweshes	243
LII.	The Lord Jesus Christ . . .	256
LIII.	The Crucifixion of our Saviour .	261

		Page
LIV.	THE DIVINITY OF CHRIST AND THE HOLY TRINITY	264
LV.	TAHRIF, OR THE ALLEGED CORRUPTION OF THE SACRED BOOKS OF THE JEWS AND CHRISTIANS . . .	267
	INDEX OF TECHNICAL TERMS . .	275

NOTES
ON
MUHAMMADANISM.

I.—MUHAMMAD.

THE earliest biographers of the Arabian Prophet, whose works are extant in Arabic, are Ibn-Isháq (A.H. 151), Ibn-Hishám (A.H. 218), Wáqidi (A.H. 207), and Tabarí (A.H. 310). Ismail Abulfida, Prince of Hamah, in Syria (A.H. 733), compiled a Life of Muhammad in Arabic, which was translated by John Gagnier, Professor of Arabic at Oxford (A.D. 1723), and into English by the Rev. W. Murray, Episcopal clergyman at Duffus, in Scotland.* Dr. Sprenger of Calcutta commenced a Life of Muham-

---

* Mr. Murray's translation was published at Elgin (without date). It is exceedingly scarce, the British Museum not possessing a copy.

mad in English, and printed the first part of it at Allahabad (A.D. 1851); but it was never completed. The learned author afterwards published his work in German in 1869.* The only Life of Muhammad in English, which has any pretension to original research, is that by Sir William Muir of the Bengal Civil Service.†

Muhammad (lit. *the praised one*), son of Abdul Muttalib, by his wife Amina, was born at Mecca, August 29th, A.D. 570. He assumed the prophetic office at the age of forty, fled from Mecca at the age of fifty-four, and died at Medinah, June 9th, A.D. 632, aged sixty-two.

The *Hijrat*, or Hegira (the flight from Mecca), which is the Muhammadan era, dates from July 16th, A.D. 622.

The character of Muhammad is an historic problem, and many have been the conjectures as to his motives and designs. Was he an impostor, a fanatic, or an honest man—" a very prophet of God?" And the problem might

---

* Das Leben und die Lehre des Mohammad. A. Sprenger. 6 vols. 8vo. Berlin, 1869.

† Life of Mahomet. 4 vols. 8vo. London, 1858-61. New Edition. 1 vol. 8vo. London, 1877.

have for ever remained unsolved had not the Prophet himself appealed to the Old and New Testament in proof of his mission. This is the crucial test, established by the Prophet himself. He claims to be weighed in the balance with the Divine Jesus. Having done so, we find him wanting.

Objection has often been made to the manner in which Christian divines have attacked the private character of Muhammad. Why reject the prophetic mission of Muhammad on account of his private vices, when you receive as inspired the sayings of a Balaam, a David, or a Solomon? We do not, as a rule, attack the character of Muhammad in dealing with Islám; it rouses opposition, and is an offensive line of argument. Still, in forming an estimate of his prophetical pretensions, we contend that the character of Muhammad is an important item in our bill of indictment. We readily admit that bad men have sometimes been, like Balaam and others, the divinely appointed organs of inspiration; but in the case of Muhammad his professed inspiration sanctioned and encouraged his own vices. That which ought to have been the fountain of purity was, in fact, the cover of the

1 A

Prophet's depravity.* But how different it is in the case of the true prophet David, where, in the words of inspiration, he lays bare to public gaze the enormity of his own crimes. The deep contrition of his inmost soul is manifest in every line—" I acknowledge my transgression and my sin is ever before me : against Thee, Thee only, have I sinned, and done this evil in Thy sight."

The best defenders of the Arabian Prophet† are obliged to admit that the matter of Zeinab, the wife of Zeid, and again, of Mary, the Coptic slave, are "an indelible stain" upon his memory; that "he is once or twice untrue to the kind and forgiving disposition of his best nature; that he is once or twice unrelenting in the punishment of his personal enemies; and that he is guilty even more than once of conniving at the assassination of inveterate opponents;" but they give no satisfactory explanation or apology for all this being done *under the supposed sanction of God* in the Qurán.

In forming an estimate of Muhammad's pro-

---

* *Vide* Qurán, chap. xxxiii. 37, and chap. lxvi. 1.

† *Vide* Muhammad and Muhammadism, by Mr. R. Bosworth Smith, M.A., an Assistant Master of Harrow School.

phetical pretensions, it must be remembered that he did not claim to be the founder of a new religion, but merely of a new covenant. He is the last and greatest of all God's prophets. He is sent to convert the world to the one true religion which God had before revealed to the five great lawgivers—Adam, Noah, Abraham, Moses, and Jesus! The creed of Muhammad, therefore, claims to supersede that of the Lord Jesus. And it is here that we take our stand. We give Muhammad credit as a warrior, as a legislator, as a poet, as a man of uncommon genius, raising himself amidst great opposition to a pinnacle of renown; we admit that he is, without doubt, one of the greatest heros the world has ever seen; but when we consider his claims to *supersede* the mission of the Divine Jesus, we strip him of his borrowed plumes, and reduce him to the condition of an impostor!* For whilst he has adopted and

---

* " There are modern biographers of the Prophet who would have us believe that he was not conscious of falsehood when making these assertions. He was under a hallucination, of course, but he believed what he said. This is to me incredible. The legends of the Koran are derived chiefly from Talmudic sources; Muhammad must

avowed his belief in the sacred books of the Jew and the Christian, and has given them all the stamp and currency which his authority and influence could impart, he has attempted to rob Christianity of every distinctive truth which it possesses—its Divine Saviour, its Heavenly Comforter, its pure code of social morals, its spirit of love and truth—and has written his own refutation and condemnation with his own hand, by professing to confirm the divine oracles which sap the very foundations of his prophetical pretensions.

---

have learned them from some Jew resident in or near Mekka. To work them up in the form of rhymed Suras, to put his own peculiar doctrines in the mouths of Jewish patriarchs, the Virgin Mary, and the infant Jesus (who talks like a good Moslem from his birth), must have required time, thought, and labour. It is not possible that the man who had done all this could have forgotten all about it, and believed that these legends had been brought to him ready prepared by an angelic visitor. Muhammad was guilty of falsehood under circumstances where he deemed the end justified the means. . . . . He was brought face to face with the question which every spiritual reformer has to consider, against which so many noble spirits have gone to ruin,—will not the end justify the means?"—"Islam under the Arabs," by Major Durie Osborn, p. 21.

We follow the would-be prophet in his self-asserted mission from the cave of Híra to the closing scene, when he dies in the midst of the lamentations of his harem, and the contentions of his friends—the visions of Gabriel, the period of mental depression, the contemplated suicide, the assumption of the prophetic office, his struggles with Meccan unbelief, his flight to Medina, his triumphant entry into Mecca—and whilst we wonder at the genius of the hero, we pause at every stage and inquire, " Is this the Apostle of God whose mission is to claim universal dominion to the suppression not merely of idolatry, but of Christianity itself?" Then it is that the divine and holy character of Jesus rises to our view, and the inquiring mind sickens at the thought of the beloved, the pure, the lowly Jesus giving place to that of the ambitious, the sensual, the *time-serving* hero of Arabia. In the study of Islam the character of Muhammad needs an apology or a defence at every stage; but in the contemplation of the Christian system, whilst we everywhere read of Jesus, and see the reflection of His image in everything we read, the heart revels in the contemplation, the inner pulsations of our spiritual life bound within us at the study of a character so divine, so pure.

We are not insensible to the beauties of the Qurán as a literary production, although they have, without doubt, been overrated; but as we admire its conceptions of the Divine nature, its deep and fervent trust in the power of God, its frequent deep moral earnestness, and its sententious wisdom, we would gladly rid ourselves of our recollections of the Prophet, his licentious harem, his sanguinary battle-fields, his ambitious schemes; whilst as we peruse the Christian scriptures we find the grand central charm in the divine character of its founder. It is the divine character of Jesus which gives fragrance to His words; it is the divine form of Jesus which shines through all He says or does; it is the divine life of Jesus which is the great central point in Gospel history. How then, we ask, can the creed of Muhammad, the son of Abdullah, supersede and abrogate that of Jesus, the Son of God? It is a remarkable coincidence that whilst the founder of Islam died feeling that he had but imperfectly fulfilled his mission,* the founder of Christianity died in the full consciousness that His work was done—" It is finished." It was in professing to produce a revelation which should supersede that of Jesus that Muhammad set the seal to his own refutation.

* Waqidi relates that Muhammad shortly before his death called for a " shoulder blade " upon which to write another chapter of the Qurán, which should prevent them going astray for ever.

II.—ISLAM.

Islá'm is the name given to the Muhammadan religion by its founder. Abdul Haqq (the commentator on the Mishkát) says it implies "submission to the divine will."

In the Dictionary of the Qurán entitled Moghrab, *Islám* is explained as "entering into peace (*salm*) with another," alluding to the fact that he who embraces Islám in a Muhammadan state becomes free from all those penalties and disabilities which belong to one who does not embrace the faith.

In the Qurán the word is used for doing homage to God. Islám is said to be the religion of all the prophets from the time of Abraham, as will appear from the following verses (Suratul-Imrán, ver. 78, 79) :—"We believe in God and in what hath been sent down to Abraham, and Ishmael, and Isaac, and Jacob, and the Tribes, and in what was given to Moses, and Jesus and the Prophets from their Lord. We make no difference between them, and to him are we resigned (*i.e. Muslims*). Whoso desireth any other religion than *Islám*, that religion shall never be accepted of him, and in the next world he shall be lost."

There are three words used by Muhammadan writers for religion, namely, *Dín, Millat*, and *Mazhab*; and in the Kitáb-ut-Tárífát the difference implied in these words is said to be as follows:—*Dín* as it stands in its relation to God, *e.g. Dín-Ullah*, the religion of God; *Millat*, as it stands in relation to a prophet or lawgiver, *e.g. Millat-i-Ibrahím*, the religion of Abraham; and *Mazhab* as it stands in relation to the divines of Islám, *e.g. Mazhab-i-Hanafí*, the religion of Hanífa. The expression *Dín*, however, is of general application.

Those who profess the religion of Islám are called Musalmáns, Muslims, or Momins.

Ahl-i-Kitáb," the people of the Book," is used for Muhammadans, Jews, and Christians.

III.—RULE OF FAITH.

THE Muhammadan rule of faith is based upon what are called the four foundations of orthodoxy, namely, the *Qurán,* or, as it is called, *Kalám Ullah,* the Word of God; the *Hadís* (pl. *Ahádís*), or the traditions of the sayings and practice of Muhammad; *Ijmá',* or the consent of the Mujtahidín, or learned doctors; and *Qiás,* or the analogical reasoning of the learned.

In studying the Muhammadan religious system it must be well understood that Islám is not simply the religion of the Qurán, but that all Muhammadans, whether Sunni, Shía'h, or Wahhábi, receive the Traditions as an authority in matters of faith and practice. The *Sunni* Muhammadans arrogate to themselves the title of traditionists; but the Shía'hs also receive the Hadís as binding upon them, although they do not acknowledge the same collection of traditions as those received by their opponents. The

Wahhábis receive the "six correct books of the Sunnis."

The *example* of Muhammad is just as binding upon the Muslim, as that of Him who said "Learn of me" is upon the Christian, and very many were the injunctions which the "Prophet" gave as to the transmission of his sayings and practice, and very elaborate is the *canon* whereby Muslims arrive at what they believe to be the example of their Prophet. If, therefore, the grand and elaborate system of morals as expressed in the law of Islám has failed to raise the standard of morality amongst the nations of the earth which have embraced its creed, it is not unreasonable to conclude that its failure rests in the absence of a living example of truth.

IV.—THE QURA'N.*

THE word *Qurán* is derived from the Arabic *Qara*, which occurs at the commencement of Súra xcv., which is said to have been the first chapter revealed to Muhammad; and has the same meaning as the Hebrew *kara*, "to read," or "to recite," which is frequently used in Jeremiah xxxvi., as well as in other places in the Old Testament. It is, therefore, equivalent to the Hebrew *mikra*, rendered in Nehemiah viii. 18. "the reading." It is the title given to the Muhammadan Scriptures which are usually appealed to and quoted from as the "*Qurán Majíd*," or the "Glorious Qurán"; the "*Qurán Sharíf*," or the "Noble Qurán"; and is also called the "*Fúrqán*," or "Distinguisher,"

---

* The contents of this article appear as an Introduction to the Roman-Urdú edition of the Qurán, published at Ludianah, North India, 1877.

"*Kalám Ulláh,*" or the "Word of God," and "*Al kitáb,*" or "the Book."*

Muhammadans believe the Qurán to be the inspired Word of God sent down to the lowest heaven complete,† and then revealed from time to time to the Prophet by the Angel Gabriel.

There is, however, only one ‡ distinct assertion in the Qurán of Gabriel having been the medium of inspiration, namely, Súra-i-Baqr (ii.), 91; and this occurs in a Medina Súra, revealed about seven years after the Prophet's rule had been established. In the Súra-i-Shura (xxvi.), 192, the Qurán is said to have been given by the "*Rúh ul A'mín,*" or Faithful Spirit; and in the Súra-i-Najm (liii.), 5, Muhammad claims to have been taught by the "*Shadíd-ul-Quá,*"

---

* According to Jalál-ud-dín Syuty there are fifty-five titles of the Qurán. (See the Itqán, p. 117.)

† See Jalál-ud-dín's Itqán, p. 91. The "Recording Angels" mentioned in the Súra-i-Abas (lxxx.), 15, are said to have written the Qurán before it was sent down from heaven.

‡ Gabriel (*Jibráíl*) is only mentioned twice by name in the Qurán: once in the verse noted above, and again in the Súra-i-Tahrím (lxvi.), 4. He is supposed to be alluded to under the title of Rúh-ul-Qudus, or the Holy Spirit, in Súras Baqr (ii.), 82, 254; Máida (v.), 109; Nahl (xvi.), 104.

or One terrible in power; and in the Traditions the agent of inspiration is generally spoken of as "an angel" (*malak*).* It is, therefore, not quite certain through what agency Muhammad believed himself to be inspired of God.

According to Ayeshah, one of the Prophet's wives, the revelation was first communicated in dreams. Ayeshah relates†:—"The first revelations which the Prophet received were in true dreams; and he never dreamt but it came to pass as regularly as the dawn of day. After this the Prophet was fond of retirement, and used to seclude himself in a cave in mount Hírâa and worship there day and night. He would, whenever he wished, return to his family at Mecca, and then go back again, taking with him the necessaries of life. Thus he continued to return to Khadíjah from time to time, until one day the revelation came down to him, and the angel (*malak*)‡ came

---

* *Malak.* Hebrew, *Malakh,* an angel; prophet; a name of office, not of nature. See Wilson's Hebrew Lexicon, p. 13.

† Mishkát, bk. xxiv. chap. v. pt. 1.

‡ Capt. Matthews, in his edition of the Mishkát, has followed the Persian Commentator, and translated the

to him and said, 'Read' (*iqaráa*); but the Prophet said, 'I am not a reader.' And the Prophet related, that he (*i. e.* the angel) took hold of me and squeezed me as much as I could bear, and he then let me go and said again, 'Read!' And I said, 'I am not a reader.' Then he took hold of me a second time, and squeezed me as much as I could bear, and then let me go, and said 'Read!' And I said, 'I am not a reader.' Then he took hold of me a third time and squeezed me as much as I could bear, and said:—

"'Read! in the name of thy Lord who created;
  Created man from a clot of blood in the womb.
"'Read! for thy Lord is the most beneficent,
  He hath taught men the use of the pen;
  He hath taught man that which he knoweth not.'*

" Then the Prophet repeated the words himself, and with his heart trembling he returned (*i. e.* from Hiráa to Mecca) to Khadíjah, and

---

word *Malak*, Gabriel, instead of Angel, and most of our English authors have quoted the tradition from his book.

* Súra-i-Alaq (xcvi.), the first five verses. The other verses of the chapter are of a later date.

said, 'Wrap me up, wrap me up.' And they wrapped him up in a garment till his fear was dispelled, and he told Khadíjah what had passed, and he said: 'Verily, I was afraid I should have died.' Then Khadíjah said, 'No, it will not be so. I swear by God, He will never make you melancholy or sad. For verily you are kind to your relatives, you speak the truth, you are faithful in trust, you bear the afflictions of the people, you spend in good works what you gain in trade, you are hospitable, and you assist your fellow men.' After this, Khadíjah took the Prophet to Waraqa, who was the son of her uncle, and she said to him, 'O son of my uncle! hear what your brother's son says.' Then Waraqa said to the Prophet, 'O son of my brother! what do you see?' Then the Prophet told Waraqa what he saw, and Waraqa said, 'That is the *Námús** which God sent to Moses.' Ayeshah also relates

---

* *Námús*. Understood by all Commentators to be the angel Gabriel. It has, however, many significations, *e.g.* Law, Voice, Sound, &c. (see Johnson's Arabic Dictionary) Probably a corruption of the Greek νόμος, which is always used in the New Testament for the Law of Moses.

that Haris-ibn-Hishám asked the Prophet, 'How did the revelation come to you?' and the Prophet said, 'Sometimes like the noise of a bell, and sometimes the angel would come and converse with me in the shape of a man.'"

According to A'yeshah's statement, the Súra-i-Alaq (xcvi.) was the first portion of the Qurán revealed; but it is more probable that the poetical Súras, in which there is no express declaration of the prophetic office, or of a divine commission, were composed at an earlier period. Internal evidence would assign the earliest date to the Súras Zilzál (xcix.), Asar (ciii.), A'diyát (c.), and Fátiha (i.), which are rather the utterances of a searcher after truth than of an Apostle of God.

The whole book was not arranged until after Muhammad's death, but it is believed that the Prophet himself divided the Súras and gave most of them their present titles, which are chosen from some word which occurs in the chapter.* The following is the

---

* The ancient Jews divided the whole Law of Moses into fifty-four Sections, which were called *Sidrah*, or an

account of the collection and arrangement of the Qurán, as it stands at present, as given in traditions recorded by Bokhárí :—

"Zaid-ibn-Sábit, relates*:—'Abú-Bakr sent a person to me, and called me to him, at the time of the battle with the people of Zemámah; and I went to him, and Omar was with him; and Abú-Bakr said to me, "Omar came to me and said, 'Verily, a great many of the readers of the Qurán were slain on the day of the battle with the people of Zemámah; and really I am afraid that if the slaughter should be great, much will be lost from the Qurán, because every person remembers something of it; and, verily, I see it advisable for you to order the Qurán to be collected into one book.' I said to Omar, 'How can I do a thing which the Prophet has not done.' He said, 'I swear by God, this collecting of the Qurán is a good thing.' And Omar used to be constantly returning to me and saying: 'You must collect the Qurán,' till at length

---

order or division. These sections had each a technical name, e.g. the first was called "Bereshith," and the second "Noah." (See Dr. Adam Clark on Genesis.)

* Mishkát, bk. viii. chap. iii. pt. 3.

God opened my breast so to do, and I saw what Omar had been advising.' And Zaid-ibn-Sábit says that, 'Abú-Bakr said to me, "You are a young and sensible man, and I do not suspect you of forgetfulness, negligence, or perfidy; and, verily, you used to write for the Prophet his instructions from above; then look for the Qurán in every place and collect it." I said, "I swear by God, that if people had ordered me to carry a mountain about from one place to another, it would not be heavier upon me than the order which Abú-Bakr has given for collecting the Qurán." I said to Abú-Bakr, "How do you do a thing which the Prophet of God did not?" He said, "By God, this collecting of the Qurán is a good act." And he used perpetually to return to me, until God put it into my heart to do the thing which the heart of Omar had been set upon. Then I sought for the Qurán, and collected it from the leaves of the date, and white stones, and the breasts of people that remembered it, till I found the last part of the chapter entitled *Tauba* (Repentance), with Abú-Khuzaimah Ansárí, and with no other person. These leaves were in the possession of Abú-Bakr, until God caused him to die; after which Omar had them in his life-time; after that, they remained with his daughter, Hafsah; after that, Osmán compiled them into one book.'

"Anas-ibn-Málik relates:—'Huzaifah came to Osmán, and he had fought with the people of Syria in the conquest of Armenia; and had fought in Azurbaiján, with the people of Irák, and he was shocked at the different ways of people reading the Qurán. And Huzaifah said to Osmán, "O Osmán, assist this people, before they differ in the Book of God, just as the Jews and Christians differ in their books." Then Osmán sent a person to Hafsah, ordering her to send those portions which she had, and saying, "I shall have a number of copies of them taken, and will then return them to you." And Hafsah sent the portions to Osmán, and Osmán ordered Zaid-ibn-Sábit, Ansárí, and Abdullah-bin-Zubair, and Said-ibn-Alnas, and Abdulláh-ibn-ul-Háris-bin-Hishám; and these were all of the Quraish tribe, except Zaid-ibn-Sábit and Osmán. And he said to the three Quraishites, "When you and Zaid-ibn-Sábit differ about any part of the dialect of the Qurán, then do ye write it in the Quraish dialect, because it came not down in the language of any tribe but theirs." Then they did as Osmán had ordered; and when a number of copies had been taken, Osmán returned the leaves to Hafsah. And Osmán sent a copy to every quarter of the countries of Islám, and ordered all other leaves to be burnt, and Ibn-Shaháb said, "Kharíjah, son of Zaid-ibn-Sábit, informed me, saying, 'I could not find one verse when I was writing the Qurán, which, verily, I heard from the Prophet; then I looked for it, and found it with Khuzaimah Ansárí, and entered it into the Súra-i-Ahzáb.'"

This recension of the Qurán produced by Khalífa Osmán has been handed down to us unaltered; and, as Sir William Muir remarks, "there is probably no other book in the world which has remained twelve centuries with so pure a text."*

That various readings (such as Christians understand by the term) did exist when Osmán produced the first uniform edition is

---

* Muir's "Life of Mohamet," vol. i. Introduction.

more than probable, and the Shi'ahs have always charged the Ansárs* with "having mutilated and changed and made the Qurán what they pleased;" a charge, however, which they do not attempt to prove, beyond the mere assertion that certain passages were omitted which favoured the claims of Alí to be the first Khalif.

The various readings (*Qira'at*) in the Qurán are not such as are usually understood by the term in English authors, but different *dialects* of the Arabic language. Ibn Abbas says the Prophet said, "Gabriel taught me to read the Qurán in one dialect, and when I recited it he taught me to recite it in another dialect, and so on until the number of dialects increased to seven." †

Muhammad seems to have adopted this expedient to satisfy the desire of the leading

---

* See the Hyát-ul-Kalúb, a Shi'ah book of Traditions, leaf 420. "The Ansárs were ordained to oppose the claims of the family of Muhammad, and this was the reason why the other wretches took the office of Khalif by force. After thus treating one Khalif of God, they then mutilated and changed the other Khalif, which is the book of God."

† Mishkát, bk. ii. chap. ii. pt. 1.

tribes to have a Qurán in their own dialect; for Abdul Haqq* says, "The Qurán was first revealed in the dialect of the Quraish, which was the Prophet's native tongue; but when the Prophet saw that the people of other tribes recited it with difficulty then he obtained permission from God to extend its currency by allowing it to be recited in all the chief dialects of Arabia, which were seven:—Quraish, Taí, Hawázin, Ahl-i-Yaman, Saqíf, Huzail, and Baní-Tamín. Every one of these tribes accordingly read the Qurán in its own dialect, till the time of Osmán, when these differences of reading were prohibited."

These seven dialects are called *Saba'ta-Ahrúf*, and the science of reading the Qurán in the correct dialect is called *'Ilm-i-Tajwíd*.

The chronological arrangement of the chapters of the Qurán is most important. In the present Urdú edition, as well as in all Arabic editions, the Súrás are placed as they must have been arranged by Zaid-ibn-i-Sábit, who put them together regardless of all chro-

---

* Abdul Haqq, the Persian Commentator of the Mishkát.

nological sequence. If, therefore, we arrange them according to the order which is given in Syuty's Itqán,* we shall not fail to mark the gradual development of Muhammad's mind from that of a mere moral teacher and reformer, to that of a prophet and warrior chief. The contrast between the earlier, middle, and later Súrás is very striking. He who at Mecca is the admonisher and persuader, at Medína is the legislator and the warrior, who dictates obedience, and uses other weapons than the pen of the poet and the scribe. When business pressed, as at Medína, poetry makes way for prose; and although touches of the poetical element occasionally break forth, and he has to defend himself up to a very late period against the charge of being merely a poet, yet this is rarely the case in the Medína Súrás, in which we so frequently meet with injunctions to obey God and the Prophet.†

To fully realize the gradual growth of Mu-

---

* The chronological list as given in Jalál-ud-dín Syuty's Itqán will be found in the Index of the Súras.

† See Rodwell's Introduction to the English Qurán, in which the Súrás are chronologically arranged.

hammad's religious system in his own mind, it is absolutely necessary to read the Qurán through, not in the order in which it now stands, but that in which Muslim divines admit that it was revealed. At the same time it must be remembered that all Muhammadan doctors allow that in most of the Súrás there are verses which belong to a different date from that of other portions of the chapter; for example, in the Súra-i-'Alaq the first five verses belong to a much earlier date than the others; and in Súra-i-Baqr, verse 234 is acknowledged by all commentators to have been revealed after verse 240, which it abrogates.

The sources whence Muhammad derived the materials for his Qurán, are, over and above the more poetical parts, which are his own creation, the legends of his time and country, Jewish traditions based upon the Talmud, perverted to suit his own purposes, and the floating Christian traditions of Arabia and South Syria. Muhammadanism, however, owes more to Judaism[*] than it does to either

---

[*] See a book by M. Geiger entitled, "Was hat Muhammed aus dem Judenthume aufgenommen," in which

Christianity or Sabeanism, for it is simply Talmudic Judaism adapted to Arabia, plus the Apostleship of Jesus and Muhammad. Wherever Muhammad departs from the monotheistic principles of Judaism, as in the idolatrous practices of the Pilgrimage to the K'aba, it is evident that it is done as a necessary concession to the national feelings and sympathies of the people of Arabia, and it is absolutely impossible for Muhammadan divines to reconcile the idolatrous rites of the K'aba with that simple monotheism which it was evidently Muhammad's intention to establish in Arabia.

The Qurán is divided into :—

1. *Harf* (pl. *Hurúf*), Letters; of which there are said to be 323,671.

2. *Kalimah* (pl. *Kalimát*), Words; of which there are 77,934.

3. *A'yat* (pl. *A'yát*), Verses. A'yát is a word which signifies "signs," and it was used

---

that learned Jew has traced all the leading features of Islám to Talmudic sources. Also "Literary Remains of Emanuel Deutsch." Essay on Islám.

by Muhammad for short sections or verses of his supposed revelation. There are said to be 6,616 verses in the whole book; but the division of verses differs in different editions of the Arabic Qurán. The number of verses in the Arabic Quráns are recorded after the title of the Súra, and the verses distinguished in the text by a small cypher or circle.*

4. *Súra* (pl. *Suwar*), Chapters. A word which signifies a row or series, but which is now used exclusively for the chapters of the Qurán, which are one hundred and fourteen in number. These chapters are called after some word which occurs in the text, and if the Traditions are to be trusted, they were so named by Muhammad himself, although the verses of their respective Súrás were undoubtedly arranged after his death, and sometimes with little regard to their sequence. Musalmán doctors admit that the Khalif Osmán arranged the chapters in the order in which they now stand in the Qurán.

---

* Unfortunately the verses in Rodwell's English Qurán do not correspond with the Arabic Quráns in use amongst the Muhammadans of India.

5. *Rukú'* (pl. *Rukúát*), Prostrations. These are of two kinds, the *Rukú'* of a Súra and the *Rukú'* of a Sípára, and are distinguished in the Arabic Qurán by the letter '*ain* on the margin. Muhammadans generally quote by the Rukú and not by the verse.

6. *Ruba'*, The quarter of a Sípára.
7. *Nisf*, The half of a Sípára.
8. *Suls*, Three-quarters of a Sípára.
9. *Sípára*,* the Persian for the Arabic *Juz*. The Sípáras or Juz, are thirty in number, and it is said that the Qurán is so divided to enable the pious Muslim to recite the whole of the Qurán in the thirty days of Ramazán. Muhammadans generally quote their Qurán by the *Sípára* and *Ruku'*, and not by the *Súra* and *A'yat*.

10. *Manzil* (pl. *manázil*), Stages. These are seven in number, and are marked by the letters F, M, Y, B, Sh, W, and Q, which words are said to spell *Famíbeshauq*, *i. e.* "My mouth with desire." They have been arranged to enable the devout Muslim to recite the whole in the course of a week.

---

* The Persian word *Sípára* is derived from *sí*, thirty, and *pára*, a portion.

THE QURAN. 31

'Ilm-i-Usúl,* or the Exegesis of the Qurán, is a science, some knowledge of which is absolutely necessary to enable the Christian controversialist to meet a Muhammadan opponent. It is used by the Muslim divine to explain away many apparent or real contradictions which exist in the Qurán, and it is also available for a similar purpose when rightly used by the Christian in explanation of the exegesis of his own sacred books.

The words (alfáz) of the Qurán are of four classes :—Kháss, 'Amm, Mushtarak, and Muawwal.

(1) Kháss, Words used in a special sense. These are of three kinds :—Khusús-ul-jins, Special genus; Khusús-un-nau', Special species; Khusús-ul-'ain, Special individuality.

(2) 'Amm, Collective or common, which embrace many individuals or things.

(3) Mushtarak, Complex words which have several significations; e.g. 'ain, a word which

---

* 'Ilm-i-Usúl embraces both the exegesis of the Qurán and Hadís. The most authoritative works on the 'Ilm-i-Usúl of the Qurán are Syuty's Itqán (Sprenger's edition), and the Manár-ul-Usúl, and its commentary the Núr-ul-Anwár.

signifies an Eye, a Fountain, the Knee, or the Sun.

(4) *Muawwal*, Words which require to be explained: *e. g. Sulát* may mean either the Liturgical daily prayer (*Namáz*), or simple prayer (*Duá'*).

II. The Sentences ('*Ibárat*) of the Qurán are either *Záhir* or *Khafí*, *i. e.* either Obvious or Hidden.

Obvious sentences are of four classes:— *Záhir, Nass, Mufassar, Muhkam*.

(1) *Záhir.*—Those sentences, the meaning of which is *Obvious* or clear, without any assistance from the context (*karína*).

(2) *Nass.*—Those sentences the meaning of which is *Manifest* from the text: *e. g.* "Take in marriage of such other women as please you, two, three, or four." Here it is manifest that the expression "such other women as please you" is restricted.

(3) *Mufassar.* — Sentences which are *explained* by some expression in the verse: *e. g.* "And the angels prostrated themselves all of them with one accord *save Iblís.*" Here

it is explained that Iblís did not prostrate himself.

(4) *Muhkam.* — Perspicuous sentences, the meaning of which is incontrovertible: *e. g.* Súra-i-Máida (v.), 98, "He (God) knoweth all things.".

Hidden sentences are either *Khafí, Mushkil, Mujmal,* or *Mutashábih.*

(1) *Khafí.*—Sentences in which other persons or things are hidden beneath the plain meaning of a word or expression contained therein : *e. g.* Súra-i-Máida (v.), 42, "As for a thief whether male or female cut ye off their hands in recompense for their doings." In this sentence the word *Sáriq,* " thief," is understood to have *hidden* beneath its literal meaning, both pickpockets and highway robbers.

(2) *Mushkil.*—Sentences which are *ambiguous*: *e. g.* Súra-i-Dahr (lxxvi.), 15, "Vessels of silver and decanters which are of glass, decanters of glass with silver whose measure they shall mete."

(3) *Mujmal.*—Sentences which are *compendious,* and have many interpretations: *e. g.*

Súra-i-Má'rij (lxx.), 19, "Man truly is by creation hasty."

(4) *Mutashábih.*—*Intricate* sentences, or expressions, the exact meaning of which it is impossible for man to ascertain until the day of resurrection, but which was known to the Prophet: *e. g.* the letters Alif, Lám, Mím (A. L. M.); Alif, Lám, Rá (A. L. R.); Alif, Lám, Mím, Rá (A. L. M. R.), etc., at the commencement of different Súras or chapters. Also Súra-i-Mulk (lxvii.) 1, "In whose hand is the Kingdom," *i. e.* God's *hand* (Arabic, *yad*); and Súra-i-Twá Há (xx.), "He is most merciful and sitteth on His throne," *i. e.* God *sitteth* (Arabic, *istawá*); and Súra-i-Baqr (ii.), 115, "The face of God" (Arabic, *waj-ullah*).

III. The use (*isti'mál*) of words in the Qurán is divided into four classes. They are either *Haqíqat, Majáz, Saríh,* or *Kináyah.*

(1) *Haqíqat.*—Words which are used in their *literal* meaning : *e. g. rukú,* a prostration; *ziná,* adultery.

(2) *Majáz.*—Words which are *figurative.*

(3) *Saríh.*—Words the meaning of which is

clear and *palpable*: *e. g.* "Thou art *free*," "Thou art *divorced.*"

(4) *Kináyah.*—Words which are *metaphorical* in their meaning: *e. g.* "Thou art *separated*; by which may be meant "thou art *divorced.*"

IV. The deduction of arguments, or *istidlál*, as expressed in the Qurán, is divided into four sections: *'Ibárat, Ishárat, Dalálat,* and *Iqtizá.*

(1) *'Ibárat.*—The plain sentence.

(2) *Ishárat.*—A sign or hint: *e. g.* "Born of him;" meaning, of course, the father.

(3) *Dalálat.*—The *argument* arising from a word or expression: *e. g.* Súra-i-Baní Isráíl (xvii.), 23, "Say not unto your parents fie" (Arabic, *uff*); from which it is *argued* that children are not either to abuse or beat their parents.

(4) *Iqtizá.*—*Demanding* certain conditions: *e. g.* Súra-i-Nisá (iv.), 91, "Whoso killeth a Mumin (believer) by mischance shall be bound to free a slave." Here the condition demanded is that the slave shall be the property of the person who frees him.

An acquaintance with the use of these

expressions used in the exegetical commentaries of the Qurán is of great assistance to the Bazaar-preacher, for it often happens that Maulavís interrupt the preacher by putting some difficult question, which the most able missionary will find it difficult to answer to the satisfaction of a mixed assemblage. For instance, an interesting discourse or discussion is often interrupted by a Maulaví putting the following question: "What did Jesus mean when He said, 'All that ever came before me were thieves or robbers?'" The sole object of the Maulaví being to interrupt a profitable conversation or sermon, the best reply to such an one would be, "Maulaví Sáhib, you know sentences are Záhir or Khafí, hidden or evident. That is Khafí. Hidden sentences you know are of four kinds, Khafí, Mushkil, Mujmal, or Mutashábih. I consider the text you have quoted to be Mujmal, and you must admit that it would take up too much time to explain a *Mujmal* sentence in the midst of my present discourse." Most probably the Maulaví will be satisfied, for the preacher has applied a little flattering unction, in supposing that the Maulaví is learned in the principles of exegesis.

We have frequently silenced a troublesome objector, who has introduced the subject of the Trinity for no other purpose than to disturb the preaching, by telling him that it was *mutashábih*, *i.e.* intricate, and at the same time asking him if he knew the meaning of *Alif Lám Mím* at the commencement of the second chapter of the Qurán. This appears to have been our blessed Lord's method with troublesome objectors: "The baptism of John: whence was it?"

It is often painful to observe how some of our native preachers will attempt to explain the sacred mysteries of our faith in the midst of an ignorant mob. Whereas learned Muslim doctors, if placed in the same position, would decline to discuss mysterious questions under such conditions. They would say, as the Christian Divine might also say, "Many things in God's word are hidden (*khafi*), and cannot be explained to such a mixed audience as this, and besides this, in speaking of the nature (*zát*) of God, there is always some fear of blasphemy (*kufr*); I prefer speaking to you on that subject alone, after the preaching is over."

Some passages of the Qurán are contradictory, and are often made the subject of attack; but it is part of the theological belief of the Muslim doctor that certain passages of the Qurán are *mansúkh*, or abrogated by verses afterwards revealed. This was the doctrine taught by the Arabian prophet in the Súra-i-Baqr (ii.), 105, "Whatever verses we (*i. e.* God) cancel or cause thee to forget, we bring a better or its like." This convenient doctrine fell in with that law of expediency which appears to be the salient feature in Muhammad's prophetical career.

In the Tafsír-i-'Azízí it is written, that abrogated (*mansúkh*) verses of the Qurán are of three kinds: (1) Where the verse has been removed from the Qurán and another given in its place; (2) Where the injunction is abrogated and the letters of the verse remain; (3) Where both the verse and its injunction are removed from the text. This is also the view of Jalál-ud-Dín, who says, that the number of abrogated verses has been variously estimated from five to five hundred, and he gives the following table of twenty verses which most commentators acknowledge to be abrogated, or *Mansúkh*, with those verses which cancel them, or are *Násikh*.*

---

* It is to be regretted that the Greek verb καταλύω, in St. Matthew v. 17, has been translated in some of the versions of the New Testament by *mansúkh*; for it gives rise to needless controversy, and conveys a wrong impression to the Muhammadan mind as to the Christian view regarding this question. According to most Greek lexicons, the Greek word means *to throw down*, or *to destroy* (as of a building), which is the meaning given to the word in our authorized English translation. Christ did not come to destroy, or to pull down, the Law and the Prophets; but we all admit that certain precepts of the Old Testament were abrogated by those of the New Testament. Indeed we further admit that the old covenant was abrogated by the new covenant of grace. "He taketh away the first that he may establish the second," Heb. x. 9.

In the Arabic translation of the New Testament, printed at Beyrut A.D. 1869, καταλύω is translated by *naqz*, "to demolish"; and in Mr. Loewenthal's Pashto translation, A.D. 1863, by *bátilawal*, "to destroy," or "render void"; and in Henry Martyn's Persian Testament, A.D. 1837, it is also translated by the Arabic *ibtál*, *i. e.* "making void." In both the Arabic-Urdú and Roman-Urdú it is unfortunately rendered *mansúkh*, a word which has a technical meaning in Muhammadan theology contrary to that implied in the word used by our Lord in Matthew v. 17.

No.	Mansúkh.	Násikh.	Subject.
1	Súra-i-Baqr (ii.), 115,	Súra-i-Baqr (ii.), 145,	The Qibla.
2	Súra-i-Baqr (ii.), 178,	Súra-i-Máida (iv.), 49,	Qisás, or Retaliation.
		{Súra-i-Baní Isráíl (xvii.), 35,}	
3	Súra-i-Baqr (ii.), 183,	Súra-i-Baqr (ii.), 187,	The Fast of Ramazán.
4	Súra-i-Baqr (ii.), 184,	Súra-i-Baqr (ii.), 185,	Fidya, or Expiation.
5	Súra-i-Ál-i-'Imrán (iii.), 102.	Súra-i-Taghábun (lxiv.), 16,	The fear of God.
6	Súra-i-Nisá (iv.), 88,	{Súra-i-Nisá (iv.), 89,}	Jihád, or war with infidels.
		{Súra-i-Tauba (ix.), 5,}	
7	Súra-i-Baqr (ii.), 216.	Súra-i-Tauba (ix.), 36,	Jihád in the Sacred months.
8	Súra-i-Baqr (ii.), 240,	Súra-i-Baqr (ii.), 234,	Provision for widows.
9	Súra-i-Baqr (ii.), 191.	Súra-i-Tauba (ix.), 5,	Slaying enemies in the Sacred Mosque.
10	Súra-i-Nisá (iv.), 14.	Súra-i-Núr (xxiv.) 2,	Imprisonment of the adulteress.
11	Súra-i-Máida (v.), 105,	Súra-i-Taláq (lxv.), 2,	Witnesses.
12	Súra-i-Anfál (vii.), 66,	Súra-i-Anfál (vii.), 67,	Jihád, or war with infidels.
13	Súra-i-Núr (xxiv.), 3,	Súra-i-Núr (xxiv.), 32,	The marriage of adulterers.
14	Súra-i-Ahzáb (xxxiii.), 52,	Súra-i-Ahzáb (xxxiii.), 49,	The Prophet's wives.
15	Súra-i-Mujádila (lviii.), 13, first part of verse.	Súra-i-Mujádila (lviii.), 13, latter part of verse.	Giving alms before assembling a council.
16	Súra-i-Mumtahina (lx.), 11,	Súra-i-Tauba (ix.), 1,	Giving money to infidels for women taken in marriage.
17	Súra-i-Tauba (ix.), 39,	Súra-i-Tauba (ix.), 92,	Jihád, or war with infidels.
18	Súra-i-Muzammil (lxxiii.), 2.	Súra-i-Muzammil (lxxiii.), 20,	The night prayer.
19	Súra-i-Núr (xxiv.), 57,	Súra-i-Núr (xxiv.), 58,	Permission to young children to enter a house.
20	Súra-i-Nisá (iv.), 7,	Súra-i-Nisá (iv.), 11,	Division of property.

Upon a careful perusal of the Qurán, it does not appear that Muhammad ever distinctly declared that it was the object of his mission either to abrogate or to destroy the teaching of the previous prophets. On the contrary, we are told that the Qurán is "A book *confirmatory* of the previous Scriptures and their *safeguard.*"*

And yet such is the anti-Christian character of Islám that it demands nothing short of the entire destruction of God's revealed will to mankind contained in the New Testament.

In dealing with serious minded Muhammadans, we should, as far as possible, abstain from attacking any real or apparent contradictions which may exist in the Qurán, and insist more upon a general comparison between the two systems :—the teaching of Jesus and the teaching of Muhammad, the position of man under the Gospel and the position of man under the Qurán, the sonship of the Christian and the servitude of the Muslim, the covenant of Grace and the covenant of Works; and endeavour to show the true seeker after Truth and Salvation, that it is impossible for the

---

* Súra-i-Máida (v.), 52.

mission of Muhammad to abrogate and supersede that of Jesus.

It must be admitted that the Qurán deserves the highest praise for its conception of the Divine nature, that it embodies much deep and noble earnestness; but still, it is not what it professes to be—it pulls down what it professes to build up, it destroys what it professes to confirm. It is not Truth, and as the counterfeit of Truth we reject it. In the Qurán we read,* "We believe in God, and that which was sent down unto us and that which was sent down to Ibráhím and Ismáíl and Isháq and Yaqúb and the Tribes, and that which was delivered to Moses and the Prophets from the Lord, and we make no distinction between any of them." And yet this very book which "makes no distinction between any of them" and which is said to be "confirmatory" of the Scriptures, ignores the Atonement, the Sacraments of Baptism and the Lord's Supper, and denies the Crucifixion of the Saviour, the Sonship of Christ and the doctrine of the Holy Trinity.

---

* Súra-i-Baqr (ii.), 136; also Súra-i-A'l-i-'Imrán (iii.), 83.

THE TITLES

OF THE

CHAPTERS OF THE QURÁN.

No.	Title of Súra.	Meaning in English.	THE CHRONOLOGICAL ORDER.		
			According to Jalál-ud-dín.	According to Rev. J.M. Rodwell.	According to Sir W. Muir.
1	Fátiha	Preface	uncertain	8	6
2	Baqr	Cow	86	91	uncertain
3	A'l-i-'Imrán	Family of Imrán.	88	97	A.H. 2 to 10.
4	Nisá	Women	91	100	uncertain
5	Máida	Table	112	114	A.H. 6 to 10.
6	Anám	Cattle	54	89	81
7	'Aráf	Aráf	38	87	91
8	'Anfál	Spoils	87	95	A.H. 2
9	Tauba	Repentance	113	113	The last
10	Yúnus	Jonah	50	84	79
11	Húd	Hud	51	75	78
12	Yúsuf	Joseph	52	77	77
13	R'ad	Thunder	95	90	89
14	Ibráhím	Abraham	71	76	80
15	Hajr	Hajr	53	57	62
16	Nahl	Bee	69	73	88
17	Baní Isráíl	Children of Israel.	49	67	87
18	Kahaf	Cave	68	69	69
19	Maryam	Mary	43	58	68
20	Twá Há	Twá Há	44	55	75
21	Ambiyá	Prophets	72	65	86
22	Hajj	Pilgrimage	103	107	85
23	Múminún	Believers	73	64	84
24	Núr	Light	102	105	A.H. 5
25	Furqán	Qurán	41	66	74
26	Sh'urá	Poets	46	56	61
27	Namal	Ant	47	68	70
28	Qasas	Story	48	79	83
29	'Ankabút	Spider	84	81	90
30	Rúm	Greeks	83	74	60
31	Luqmán	Luqmán	56	82	50

THE QURAN.

No.	Title of Súra.	Meaning in English.	The Chronological Order.		
			According to Jalál-uddín.	According to Rev. J.M. Rodwell.	According to Sir W. Muir.
32	Sijda	Prostration	74	70	44
33	Ahzáb	Confederates	89	103	uncertain
34	Sabá	Saba	57	85	49
35	Maláika	Angels	42	86	66
36	Yá Sín	Yá Sín	40	60	67
37	Sáffát	Ranks	55	50	59
38	Swád	Swád	37	59	73
39	Zamár	Troops	58	80	45
40	Múmin	Believer	59	78	72
41	Fussilat	Explanation	60	71	53
42	Shorí	Council	61	83	71
43	Zukhráf	Jewels	62	61	76
44	Dukhán	Smoke	63	53	58
45	Jásiya	Kneeling	64	72	57
46	Ahqáf	Ahqáf	65	88	64
47	Muhammad	Muhammad	94	96	uncertain
48	Fatah	Victory	111	108	A.H. 6
49	Hujrát	Chambers	106	112	uncertain
50	Qáf	Qáf	33	54	56
51	Záriát	Breath of Winds.	66	43	63
52	Túr	Mountain	75	44	55
53	Najam	Star	22	46	43
54	Qamar	Moon	36	49	48
55	Rahmán	Merciful	96	48	40
56	Wáqia'	Inevitable	45	45	41
57	Hadíd	Iron	93	99	uncertain
58	Mujádila	Disputer	105	106	uncertain
59	Hashar	Assembly	101	102	A.H. 4
60	Mumtahiná	Proof	90	110	A.H. 7
61	Saf	Array	110	98	uncertain
62	Jum'a	Assembly	108	94	uncertain
63	Munáfiqún	Hypocrites	104	104	A.H. 65
64	Taghábun	Deceit	109	93	82
65	Taláq	Divorce	108	101	uncertain
66	Tahrím	Prohibition	107	109	A.H. 7 to 8
67	Mulk	Kingdom	76	63	42
68	Qalam	Pen	2	17	52
69	Háqa	Inevitable-Day	77	42	51
70	Ma'árij	Steps	78	47	37
71	Núh	Noah	70	51	54

THE QURAN.

No.	Title of Súra.	Meaning in English.	THE CHRONOLOGICAL ORDER.		
			According to Jalál-ud-dín.	According to Rev. J. M. Rodwell.	According to Sir W. Muir.
72	Jinn	Genii	39	62	65
73	Muzzammil	Wrapped up	3	3	46
74	Muddassir	Mantle	4	2	21
75	Qiyámat	Resurrection	30	40	36
76	Dahr	Man	97	52	35
77	Mursalát	Messengers	32	36	34
78	Nabá	News	79	37	33
79	Názi'át	Ministers of Vengeance.	80	35	47
80	'Abas	He frowned	23	24	26
81	Takwír	Folding up	6	32	27
82	Infitár	Cleaving asunder.	81	31	11
83	Tatfíf	Short Measure	85	41	32
84	Inshiqáq	Rending in sunder.	82	33	28
85	Burúj	Celestial Signs	26	28	31
86	Táriq	Night Star	35	22	29
87	'A'la	Most High	7	25	23
88	Gháshiya	Overwhelming	67	38	25
89	Fajr	Day-break	9	39	14
90	Balad	City	34	18	15
91	Shams	Sun	25	23	4
92	Lail	Night	8	16	12
93	Zuhá	Sun in his meridian.	10	4	16
94	Inshiráh	Expanding	11	5	17
95	Tín	Fig	27	26	8
96	'Alaq	Congealed blood.	1	1	19
97	Qadar	Night of power.	24	92	24
98	Baiyana	Evidence	99	21	uncertain
99	Zilzál	Earthquake	92	30	3
100	'Adiyát	Swift horses	13	34	2
101	Qári'a	Striking	29	29	7
102	Takásur	Multiplying	15	15	9
103	'Asar	Afternoon	12	27	1
104	Hamza	Slanderer	31	13	10
105	Fíl	Elephant	18	19	13
106	Qoreish	Qoreish	28	20	5

No.	Title of Súra.	Meaning in English.	The Chronological Order.		
			According to Jalál-ud-dín.	According to Rev. J. M. Rodwell.	According to Sir W. Muir.
107	Máún	Necessaries	16	14	39
108	Kausar	Kausar	14	9	18
109	Kafirún	Infidels	17	12	38
110	Nasr	Assistance	101	111	30
111	Lahab	Lahab	5	11	22
112	Ikhlás	Unity	21	10	20
113	Falaq	Day-break	19	6	uncertain
114	Nás	Men	20	7	uncertain

V.—INSPIRATION.

ACCORDING to Muhammadan theologians, inspiration is of two kinds, *Wáhí* and *Ilhám*. *Wáhí*, is that which was given to the prophets, and is used especially for the Qurán; *Ilhám* being the inspiration to *Walis*, or saints.

Ilhám is the word generally used by Christian missionaries for the inspiration of the sacred Scriptures, and we believe it is sometimes used by Arabic divines for a higher form of inspiration, but always in the compound form of *Ilhám Rabbáni*.

Shaikh Ahmad in his book, the Núr-ul-Anwár, defines inspiration as follows:—"*Wáhí*, or inspiration, is either *Záhir* (external), or *Bátin* (internal). *Wáhí Záhir* is divided into three classes:—(1) *Wáhí Qurán*, that which was given by the mouth of the angel Gabriel, and which reached the ear of the Prophet after he knew that it was Gabriel who spoke to him. (2) *Ishárat-ul-Malak*, that which was received from Gabriel, but not by word of mouth, as when the Prophet said, "The Holy Ghost has breathed into my heart." (3) *Ilhám*, or *Wáhí Qalb*, that which was made known to the Prophet by the light of prophecy. This kind of inspiration is possessed by Walis or saints, but in their case it may be true or false. *Wáhí Bátin* is that which the Prophet obtained by analogical reasoning (*qiás*) just as the enlightened doctors, or *Mujtahidín*, obtain it."

The *Ishárat-ul-Malak*, mentioned in the above quotation is never used for the inspiration of the Qurán, but for certain instructions which Muhammad professes to have received direct from Gabriel, and which are recorded in the *Hadís*, or Traditions.

Whatever may have been the actual impression upon Muhammad's mind as to the nature of the communications he professed to have received from God, it is evident that Muslim theologians have no conception of the Word of God being given in the form of the Old and New Testament Scriptures. The most plausible objection raised against the New Testament, by Muhammadan controversialists of the present day is, that the Christians have lost the original Gospels and that our present book contains merely the *Hadís*, or traditions, of Matthew, Mark, Luke, and John. It is, therefore, necessary to correct their common idea that the Gospel was revealed to Jesus in the same manner as the Qurán is said to have been given to Muhammad; to show that it was the special office of the Holy Spirit to give the New Testament Scriptures, and that they came to man by the same method of inspiration whereby the Old Testament writings were given to the Prophets of old, the Qurán being an exception to God's *usual* method of giving inspired writings to his Prophets.*

---

* *Vide* 2 Tim. iii. 16 : πᾶσα γραφὴ Θεόπνευστος "all scripture is God-breathed" (*divinatus inspirata*, Vulg.), which Dean Alford says is the idea common to the Jews. *Vide* Jos. contra Apion. i. 7.

VI.—THE TRADITIONS.

The *Hadís* (pl. *Ahádís*) is, as we have already remarked; the second part of the Muhammadan rule of faith. It forms the body of that oral law of the Arabian legislator which stands next to the Qurán in point of authority, being considered by all Muhammadans, whether Sunní, Shía'h, or Wahhábi, as a supplement to that book. The collections of these traditions are called *Hadís*, being records of the sayings of the Prophet, but they are also called *Sunna*, a word which signifies custom, or regulation.

Muhammad gave very special injunctions respecting the faithful transmission of his sayings; for example, it is related by Tirmizi, that the Prophet said, "Convey to other persons none of my words except those which ye know of a surety. Verily he who purposely represents my words wrongly, would find a place nowhere for himself but in fire."

But notwithstanding the severe warning given by Muhammad himself, it is admitted by all Muslim divines that very many spurious traditions have been handed down. Abu Dáud received only four thousand eight hundred, out of five hundred thousand, and even after this *careful* selection he states that he has mentioned "*those which seem to be authentic and those which are nearly so.*" Out of forty thousand persons who have been instrumental in handing down traditions of "the Prophet," Bokhárí only acknowledged two thousand as reliable authorities. It will, therefore, be seen how unreliable are the traditions of Islám although they are part of the rule of faith. Such being the case, it is not surprising that '*Ilm-i-Hadís*, or the Science of Tradition, has become a most important branch of Muslim Divinity, and that the following canons have been framed for the reception or rejection of traditions.

I. With reference to the character of those who have handed down the tradition * :—

(1) *Hadís-i-Sahíh,* a *genuine* tradition, is one which has been handed down by truly pious persons who have been distinguished for their integrity.

(2) *Hadís-i-Hasan,* a *mediocre* tradition, is one the narrators of which do not approach in moral excellence to those of the Sahíh class.

(3) *Hadís-i-Z'aíf,* a *weak* tradition, is one whose narrators are of questionable authority.

The disputed claims of narrators to these three classes have proved a fruitful source of learned discussion, and very numerous are the works written upon the subject.

II. With reference to the original relators of the Hadís :—

(1) *Hadís-i-Marfu',* an *exalted* tradition, is a saying, or an act, related or performed by

---

* In the first edition of these Notes the canons for the reception and rejection of traditions were taken from Sayyad Ahmad Khan's "Essay on Traditions," but in the present edition they have been arranged according to the Arabic treatise, entitled Nukhbat-al-Faqr by Shekh Shaháb-ud-dín Ahmad, edited by Capt. W. Nassau Lees, LL.D. (Calcutta, 1862.)

the Prophet himself and handed down in a tradition.

(2) *Hadís-i-Mauquf*, a *restricted* tradition, is a saying or an act related or performed by one of the *ashab* or companions of the Prophet.

(3) *Hadís-i-Maqtu'*, an *intersected* tradition, is a saying or an act related or performed by one of the *Tába'ín*, or those who conversed with the companions of the Prophet.

III. With reference to the links in the chain of the narrators of the tradition, a Hadís is either *Muttasil*, connected, or *Munqata'*, disconnected. If the chain of narrators is complete from the time of the first utterance of the saying or performance of the act recorded to the time that it was written down by the collector of traditions, it is *Muttasil*; but if the chain of narrators is incomplete, it is *Munqata'*.

IV. With reference to the manner in which the tradition has been narrated, and transmitted down from the first:—

(1) *Hadís-i-Mutawátir*, an *undoubted* tradition, is one which is handed down by very many distinct chains of narrators, and which has been always accepted as authentic and genuine, no doubt ever having been raised

against it. The learned doctors say there are only five such traditions; but the exact number is disputed.

(2) *Hadís-i-Mashhúr*, a *well-known* tradition, is one which has been handed down by at least three distinct lines of narrators. It is called also *Mustafíz*, diffused. It is also used for a tradition which was at first recorded by one person, or a few individuals, and afterwards became a popular tradition.

(3) *Hadís-i-'Azíz*, a *rare* tradition, is one related by only two lines of narrators.

(4) *Hadís-i-Gharíb*, a *poor* tradition, is one related by only one line of narrators.

Khabar-i-Wáhid, a *single saying*, is a term also used for a tradition related by one person and handed down by one line of narrators. It is a disputed point whether a *Khabar-i-Wáhid* can form the basis of Muslim doctrine.

Hadís-i-Mursal (lit. "a tradition let loose"), is a tradition which any collector of traditions, such as Bokhári and others, records with the assertion, "*the Apostle of God said.*"

Riwáyat, is a Hadís which commences with the words "*it is related,*" without the authority being given.

Hadís-i-Mauzu', an *invented* tradition, is one the *untruth* of which is beyond dispute.

It is an universal canon that no tradition can be received which is contrary to the Qurán, and it is related that when 'Ayeshah heard Omar say that Muhammad had taught that the dead could hear, she rejected the tradition as spurious, because it was contrary to the teaching of the Qurán.

Whatever may be the difference of opinion as to the authority of the various traditions, it must be remembered that they form the groundwork of the different schools of thought of the Muhammadan religion. It is, therefore, impossible for European critics to form a just estimate of the Muhammadan creed without being acquainted with those traditions which are generally received as authentic and genuine.

European writers are unfortunately under the impression that the "Muhammadan revival" is a going back to "first principles," as expressed in the Qurán, whereas, it is, as we have already remarked, a revival of the study of the traditions concerning their Prophet, which study has undoubtedly been promoted by the establishment of printing presses in Egypt,

Turkey, and India. Not that we think Islám will present any fairer proportions even when deprived of those excrescences which are supposed to have been the preternatural growth of tradition, as long as the Pilgrimage has the so-called divine sanction of the Qurán, and the position of women is regulated by the same "divine oracles."

The following are the six principal collectors of Hadís received by the Sunni Muhammadans :—

1. Muhammad Ismail *Bokhári*.*

   Born, A.H. 194; died, A.H. 256.

2. *Muslim*-ibn-i-Hajjáj.

   Born, A.H. 204; died, A.H. 261.

3. Abu Isa' Muhammad *Tirmízí*.

   Born, A.H. 209; died, A.H. 279.

4. *Abu Dáud* Sajistaní.

   Born, A.H. 202; died, A.H. 275.

5. Abu Abdur Rahmán *Nasaí*.

   Born, A.H. 215; died, A.H. 303.

6. Abu Abdullah Muhammad *Ibn-i-Májah*.

   Born, A.H. 209; died, A.H. 273.

---

* The names in *italics* denote the usual title of the book.

Some divines substitute the following for that of *Ibn-i-Májah.*

Muawattáa Imám Málik.

Born, A.H. 95; died, A.H. 179.

The following are the collections of Hadís received by the Shía'h :—

1. The *Káfi*, by Abu Jáfar Muhammad, A.H. 329.
2. The *Man-lá-yastahzirah-al-Faqíh*, by Shekh 'Ali, A.H. 381.
3. The *Tahzíb*, by Shekh Abu Jáfar Muhammad, A.H. 466.
4. The *Istibsár*, by the same author.
5. The *Nahaj-ul-Balághat*, by Sayyud Razi, A.H. 406.

Copies of the *Sihah-Sittah*, or "six correct" bocks of tradition received by the Sunnís, together with the seventh work by Imám Málik, have been lithographed, and can be purchased in the book shops of Delhi, Lucknow, and Bombay; but the work most read is the Mishkát-ul-Musábíh (the niche for lamps), which is a collection of the most reliable traditions. This work was originally in Arabic; but it was translated into Persian in the reign of Akbar. It was rendered into English by Captain Matthews, and published in Calcutta in 1809. The English translation has been long since out of print, but efforts are being made by the author of these notes for its republication. The popular collection of Shía'h traditions arranged in the form of an historical narrative is the Hyát-ul-Qulub, a Persian work which has been translated by the Rev. J. L. Merrick (Phillips, Sampson & Co., Boston, U.S., 1850).

The most trustworthy of the various collections of Sunni traditions is the one usually called *Bokhárí*. It was compiled by Abu Abdullah Muhammad ibn-i-Ismaíl a native of Bokhára. In obedience to instructions he is said to have received in a vision, he set himself to commence the collection of all the current traditions relating to Muhammad. He succeeded in collecting not fewer than six hundred thousand traditions, of which he selected only 7275 as trustworthy! These he recorded in his work; but it is said that he repeated a two *rik'at* prayer before he wrote down any one of the 7275 traditions which he recorded. There is, therefore, every reason to believe that the compilers of the books of tradition were sincere and honest in their endeavours to produce correct and well authenticated traditions of their Prophet's precepts and practice; but, as Sir William Muir remarks, "the exclusively oral character of the early traditions deprives them of every check against the licence of error and fabrication."

Sir William Muir has very ably dwelt upon the unsatisfactory character of Muhammadan tradition in the first volume of his "Life of Mahomet," to which Sayyid Ahmad Khán has written a reply in a supplement to his essay on Muhammadan tradition. The learned Sayyid is in this, as in almost everything he writes on the subject of religion, his own refutation. Sir William Muir reveals to the public "the higgledy-piggledy condition, the unauthenticity and the spuriousness of Muhammadan traditions," and surely Sayyid Ahmad Khán does but confirm the same when he writes: "All learned Muhammadan divines of every period have declared that the Qurán only is the Hadees *mutawátir*; but some doctors have declared certain other Hadeeses also to be Mutawátir, the number, however, of such Hadeeses not exceeding *five. Such are the Hadeeses that are implicitly believed, and ought to be religiously observed."*

But although the traditions of Muhammad are shrouded with a degree of uncertainty which is perplexing, not to say vexatious, to the student of history, still there can be no doubt as to the place they were intended to, and still do occupy in the theological structure of Islám. The example of Muhammad is just as binding upon the Muslim as that of our Divine Lord and Saviour is upon the Christian. And everything Muhammad said with reference to religious dogmas and morals is believed to have been inspired by God; by a "*wáhí ghair-i-mutlu'*," or an inspiration similar in kind to that which we believe to have been given to the inspired writers of our Christian Scriptures.

VII.—IJMA'.

IJMA' is the third foundation of the Muhammadan rule of faith. It literally means *collecting*, or *assembling*, and in Muslim divinity it expresses the unanimous consent of the Mujtahidín (learned doctors); or, as we should call it, "the unanimous consent of the Fathers." A Mujtahid is a Muslim divine of the highest degree of learning, a title usually conferred by Muslim rulers. There are three foundations of *Ijma'*: (1) *Itifáq-i-Qauli*, unanimous consent expressed in declaration of *opinion*; (2) *Itifáq-i-Fi'li*, expressed in unanimity of *practice*; (3) *Itifáq-i-Saqúti*, when the majority of the Mujtahidín signified their tacit assent to the opinions of the minority by "*silence*" or non-interference.

The Mujtahidín, capable of making *Ijma'*, must be "men of learning and piety, not heretics, nor fools, but men of judgment."

There is great diversity of opinion as to up to what period in the history of Islám,

Ijma' can be accepted. Some doctors assert that only the *Ijma'* of the Mujtahidín who were Asháb (companions); others, that of those who were not only "companions" but descendants" of the "Prophet," can be accepted; whilst others accept the *Ijma'* of the *Ansárs*, (helpers,) and of the *Muhájarín*, (fugitives,) who were dwellers in Medina with Muhammad. The majority of learned Muslim divines, however, appear to think that *Ijma'* may be collected in every age, although they admit that, owing to the numerous divisions which have arisen amongst Muhammadans, it has not been possible since the days of the *Taba' Taba'ín*, (*i.e.*, the followers of the followers of the companions).

The following is considered to be the relative value of *Ijma'*:—

That of the *Asháb* (companions) is equal to *Hadís Mutawátir*. That which was decided afterwards, but in accordance with the unanimous opinion of the Asháb, is equal to *Hadís Khabar-i-Mashhúr*, and that upon which there was diversity of opinion amongst the *Asháb*, but has since been decided by the later Mujtahidín is equal to *Hadís-i-Khabar-i-Wáhid*.

Amongst the Shía'hs, we believe, there are still *Mujtahidín* whose *Ijma'* is accepted, but the Sunnís have four orthodox schools of interpretation, named after their respective founders, Hanafí, Sháfa'i, Máliki, and Hambali. The Wahhábis for the most part reject Ijma' collected after the death of " the Companions."

From these remarks, it will be easily understood what a fruitful source of religious dissension and sectarian strife this third foundation of the rule of faith is. Divided as the Christian Church is by its numerous sects, it will compare favourably with Muhammadanism even in this respect. Muhammad, it is related, prophesied that as the Jewish Church had been divided into seventy-one sects! and the Christians into seventy-two! so his followers would be divided into seventy-three sects*; but every Muslim historian is obliged to admit that they have far exceeded the limits of Muhammad's prophecy; for, according to Abdul Qádir Jiláni, there are at least 150.

---

* The seventy-three sects are, according to some writers, distributed as follows:—Shia'h 31, M'utazilah 21, Khawárij 7, Murjíah 5, Najáriah 3, Jabariyah 2, Mushabiyah 1, and Nájíah (the term used for the orthodox).

VIII.—QIAS.

Qi'a's (lit. "to compare") is the fourth foundation of Islám, and expresses the analogical reasoning of the learned with regard to the teaching of the Qurán, Hadís, and Ijma'.

There are four conditions of Qiás: (1) That the precept or practice upon which it is founded must be of common (*'amm*) and not of special (*kháss*) application; (2) The cause (*illat*) of the injunction must be known and understood; (3) The decision must be based upon either the Qurán, the Hadís, or the Ijma'; (4) The decision arrived at must not be contrary to anything declared elsewhere in the Qurán and Hadís.

Qiás is of two kinds, *Qiás-i-Jalí* or evident, and *Qiás-i-Khafí* or hidden.

An example of *Qiás-i-Jalí* is as follows:—Wine is forbidden in the Qurán under the word *Khamar*, which literally means anything intoxicating; it is, therefore, evident that opium and all intoxicating drugs are also forbidden. *Qiás-i-Khafí* is seen in the following example:—In the Hadís it is enjoined that one goat in forty must be given to God. To some poor persons the money may be more acceptable; therefore, the value of the goat may be given instead of the goat.

IX.—FAITH.

FAITH, I'mán, is defined as "the belief of the heart and the confession of the mouth." It is of two kinds—*I'mán-i-Mujmal* and *I'mán-i-Mufassal*.

I'mán-i-Mujmal is a simple expression of faith in the teaching of the Qurán and the Hadís.

I'mán-i-Mufassal is a belief in the six articles of faith, viz. :—1. The Unity of God. 2. The Angels. 3. The Books. 4. The Prophets. 5. The Day of Judgment. 6. Predestination, or the Decrees of God.

X.—ALLAH OR GOD.

THE name of the Creator of the universe in the Qurán is *Allah*, which is the title given to the Supreme Being by Muhammadans of every race and language. It is called the special, or essential, name of God, the *ism-i-zát*; all other names being considered merely *ism-i-safát*, or attributes, of which there are said to be ninety-nine.* It is supposed to have been derived from the word *iláh*, a deity or god, with the addition of the definite article *al*, thus *Al-iláh*, *The* God. But Imám Hanífa says that, just as God's essence is unchangeable so is His name, and that *Alláh* has always been the name of the great Eternal Being (*vide* Ghyás-ul-Loghát). It appears to be an Arabic rendering of the Hebrew אל *el*, God. It is expressed in Per-

---

* *Vide* the ninety-nine names of God in the article on Zikr. There is also the *Ism-ul-'Azam*, the exalted name of God, which is said to be unknown.

5 A

sian and Hindustani by the word *Khudá*, derived from the Persian *Khud* (*self*); the self-existing one.

The Muhammadan belief in the existence of God is expressed in the first part of the well known confession of faith, *La-iláha Il-lal-láho*, "There is no deity but God," the interpretation of which occupies so prominent a place in all treatises of divinity.

The following is an interpretation of the Muslim belief in the existence and nature of God, by the famous scholastic divine, Imám Ghazáli, in his book entitled Al Maqsud-ul-asná, an extract from which Ockley has translated from Pocock's Specimen Historiæ Arabum:—

"Praise be to God the Creator and Restorer of all things; who does whatsoever he pleases, who is Master of the glorious throne and mighty force, and directs his sincere servants into the right way and the straight path; who favoureth them, who have once borne testimony to the unity, by preserving their confessions from the darkness of doubt and hesitation; who directs them to follow his chosen apostle, upon whom be the blessing and peace of God; and to go after his most honourable companions, to whom he hath vouchsafed his assistance and direction which is revealed to them in his essence and operations by the excellencies of his attributes, to the knowledge whereof no man attains but he that hath been taught by hearing. To these, as touching his essence, he maketh known that he is one, and hath no partner; singular, without anything like him; uniform, having no contrary; separate, having no equal. He is ancient, having no first; eternal, having no beginning; remaining for ever, having no end; continuing to eternity, without any termination. He persists, without ceasing to be; remains without falling, and never did cease, nor ever shall cease to be described by glorious attributes, nor is subject to any decree so as to be determined by any precise limits or set times, but is the First and the Last, and is within and without.

" *(What God is not.)* He, glorified be his name, is not a body endued with form, nor a substance circumscribed with limits or determined by measure; neither does he resemble bodies, as they are capable of being measured or divided. Neither is he a substance, neither do substances exist in him; neither is he an accident, nor do accidents exist in him. Neither is he like to anything that exists, neither is anything like to him; nor is he determinate in quantity nor comprehended by bounds, nor circumscribed by the differences of situation, nor contained in the heavens. He sits upon the throne, after that manner which he himself hath described, and in that same sense which he himself means, which is a sitting far removed from any notion of contact, or resting upon, or local situation; but both the throne itself, and whatsoever is upon it, are sustained by the goodness of his power, and are subject to the grasp of his hand. But he is above the throne, and above all things, even to the utmost ends of the earth; but so above as at the same time not to be a whit nearer the throne and the heaven; since he is exalted by (infinite) degrees above the throne no less than he is exalted above the earth, and at the same time is near to everything that hath a being; nay, 'nearer to man than their jugular veins, and is witness to everything:'* though

---

* *Vide* Qurán.

his nearness is not like the nearness of bodies, as neither is his essence like the essence of bodies. Neither doth he exist in anything, neither doth anything exist in him; but he is too high to be contained in any place, and too holy to be determined by time; for he was before time and place were created, and is now after the same manner as he always was. He is also distinct from the creatures by his attributes, neither is there anything besides himself in his essence, nor is his essence in any other besides him. He is too holy to be subject to change, or any local motion; neither do any accidents dwell in him, nor any contingencies befall him; but he abides through all generations with his glorious attributes, free from all danger of dissolution. As to the attribute of perfection, he wants no addition of his perfection. As to being, he is known to exist by the apprehension of the understanding; and he is seen as he is by an ocular intuition, which will be vouchsafed out of his mercy and grace to the holy in the eternal mansion, completing their joy by the vision of his glorious presence.

" *(His power.)* He, praised be his name, is

living, powerful, mighty, omnipotent, not liable to any defect or impotence; neither slumbering nor sleeping, nor being obnoxious to decay or death. To him belongs the kingdom, and the power, and the might. His is the dominion, and the excellency, and the creation, and the command thereof. The heavens are folded up in his right hand, and all creatures are couched within his grasp. His excellency consists in his creating and producing, and his unity in communicating existence and a beginning of being. He created men and their works, and measured out their maintenance and their determined times. Nothing that is possible can escape his grasp, nor can the vicissitudes of things elude his power. The effects of his might are innumerable, and the objects of his knowledge infinite.

" *(His knowledge.)* He, praised be his name, knows all things that can be understood, and comprehends whatsoever comes to pass, from the extremities of the earth to the highest heavens. Even the weight of a pismire could not escape him either in earth or heaven; but he would perceive the creeping of the black pismire in the dark night upon the hard stone, and discern the motion of an atom in the open air. He knows what is secret and conceals it, and views the conceptions of the minds, and the motions of the thoughts, and the inmost recesses of secrets, by a knowledge ancient and eternal, that never ceased to be his attribute from eternal eternity, and not by any new knowledge, superadded to his essence, either inhering or adventitious.

" *(His will.)* He, praised be his name, doth will those things to be that are, and disposes of all accidents. Nothing passes in the empire, nor the kingdom, neither little nor much, nor small nor great, nor good nor evil, nor profitable nor hurtful, nor faith nor infidelity, nor knowledge nor ignorance, nor prosperity nor adversity, nor increase nor decrease, nor obedience nor rebellion, but by his determinate counsel and decree, and his definite sentence and will. Nor doth the wink of him that seeth, nor the subtlety of him that thinketh, exceed the bounds of his will; but it is he who gave all things their beginning; he is the creator and restorer, the sole operator of what he pleases; there is no reversing his decree nor delaying what he hath determined, nor is there any refuge to man from his rebellion against him, but only his help and mercy; nor hath any man any power to perform any duty towards him, but through his love and will. Though men, genii, angels and devils, should conspire together either to put one single atom in motion, or cause it to cease its motion, without his will and approbation they would not be able to do it. His will subsists in his essence amongst the rest of his attributes, and was from eternity one of his eternal attributes, by which he willed from eternity the existence of those things that he had decreed, which were produced in their proper seasons according to his eternal will, without any *before* or *after*, and in agreement both with his knowledge and will, and not by methodising of thoughts, nor waiting for a proper time, for which reason no one thing is in him a hindrance from another.

" *(His hearing and sight.)* And he, praised be his name, is hearing and seeing, and heareth and seeth. No audible object, how still soever, escapeth his hearing; nor is any thing visible so small as to escape his sight; for distance is no hindrance to his hearing, nor darkness to his sight. He sees without pupil or eyelids, and hears without any passage or ear, even as he knoweth without a heart, and performs his actions without the assistance of any corporeal limb, and creates without any instrument, for his attributes (or properties) are not like those of men, any more than his essence is like theirs.

"*(His word.)* Furthermore, he doth speak, command, forbid, promise, and threaten by an eternal, ancient word, subsisting in his essence. Neither is it like to the word of the creatures, nor doth it consist in a voice arising from the commotion of the air and the collision of bodies, nor letters which are separated by the joining together of the lips or the motion of the tongue. The Koran, the Law, the Gospel, and the Psalter, are books sent down by him to his apostles, and the Koran, indeed, is read with tongues, written in books, and kept in hearts; yet as subsisting in the essence of God, it doth not become liable to separation and division whilst it is transferred into the hearts and the papers. Thus Moses also heard the Word of God without voice or letter, even as the saints behold the essence of God without substance or accident. And that since these are his attributes, he liveth and knoweth, is powerful and willeth and operateth, and seeth and speaketh, by life and knowledge, and will and hearing, and sight and word, not by his simple essence.

"*(His works.)* He, praised be his name, exists after such a manner that nothing besides him hath any being but what is produced by his operation, and floweth from his justice after the best, most excellent, most perfect, and most just model. He is, moreover, wise in his works, and just in his decrees. But his justice is not to be compared with the justice of men. For a man may be supposed to act unjustly by invading the possession of another; but no injustice can be conceived of God, inasmuch as there is nothing that belongs to any other besides himself, so that wrong is not imputable to him as meddling with things not appertaining to him. All things, himself only excepted, genii, men, the devil, angels, heaven, earth, animals, plants, substance, accident, intelligible, sensible, were all created originally by him. He created them by his power out of mere privation, and brought them into light, when as yet they were nothing at all, but he alone existing from eternity, neither was there any other with him. Now he created all things in the beginning for the manifestation of his power, and his will, and the confirmation of his word, which was true from all eternity. Not that he stood in need of them, nor wanted them; but he manifestly declared his glory in creating, and producing, and commanding, without being under any obligation, nor out of necessity. Loving kindness, and to show favour, and grace, and beneficence, belong to him; whereas it is in his power to pour forth upon men a variety of torments, and afflict them with various kinds of sorrows and diseases, which, if he were to do, his justice could not be arraigned, nor would he be chargeable with injustice. Yet he rewards those that worship him for their obedience on account of his promise and beneficence, not of their merit nor of necessity, since there is nothing which he can be tied to perform; nor can any injustice be supposed in him, nor can he be under any obligation to any person whatsoever. That his creatures, however, should be bound to serve him, ariseth from his having declared by the tongues of the prophets that it was due to him from them. The worship of him is not simply the dictate of the understanding, but he sent messengers to carry to men his commands, and promises, and threats, whose veracity he proved by manifest miracles, whereby men are obliged to give credit to them in those things that they relate."

XI.—ANGELS.

THE existence of angels (*malak*, pl. *maláik*), and their purity, are absolutely required to be believed in by the Qurán, and he is reckoned an infidel who denies that there are such beings, or hates any of them or asserts any distinction of the sexes. The Muhammadans reckon four archangels : (1) *Jibráíl* (Gabriel), who is God's messenger; (2) *Mikáíl* (Michael), who is the protector of the Jews; (3) *Isráfíl*, who will sound the last trumpet at the resurrection; (4) *Azráíl*, the angel of death. Muhammad undoubtedly obtained the names of these archangels from the Scriptures and Jewish tradition, although in the Apocryphal Book of Enoch* the names of the six archangels are *Uriel, Raphael, Raguel, Michael, Sarakiel,*

---

* Book of Enoch translated by Archbishop Laurence, chap. xx.

Gabriel—a fact which may be cited as an additional proof, that when Muhammad availed himself of Jewish traditions, he quoted or adopted them with the same want of accuracy as when he appealed to the Divine word of God.

There are also the two recording angels called the *Mua'qqibát*, or the angels who continually succeed each other, who record the good and evil actions of a man, one standing at his right hand and another on his left. These are also called the *Kirám-ul-Kátibín* (the exalted writers). The angel who has charge of Heaven is *Rezwán* and the angel who presides over Hell is *Málik*.

Munkar and *Nakír* are described by Muhammad as two black angels with blue eyes who visit every man in his grave, make him sit up, and examine him as to his faith in God and in Muhammad his prophet. If the answer is satisfactory, he will be allowed to sleep on in peace, but if he replies that he knows nothing of "*God's Apostle,*" then he will be struck with an iron hammer called *Mitraqat*, and he will roar out, and his cries will be heard by all animals that may be near his grave, excepting men and genii.* This exciting ceremony is said to take place as soon as the funeral party have proceeded forty paces from the grave! †

Enlightened Muhammadans of the present day attempt to explain all this in a figurative sense, but in vain, for there is a very trustworthy tradition, recorded both by *Bokhári* and *Muslim*, to the effect that Muhammad related that he himself heard the infliction of torment on infidels in their graves when passing through the grave-yard, and that his camel was frightened by their groans! This is one of the many instances of Muhammad's superstitious belief which the more recent Muhammadan divines endeavour to explain in a metaphorical sense. We have, however, shown in a previous article that the traditions of *Bokhári* are of considerable historical weight, so that there can be little doubt that Muhammad believed "*the punishments of the grave*" to be real and literal, which is opposed to the teaching of God's revealed word (*vide* Eccl. ix. 10; xii. 7; Psalm cxlvi. 4).

---

* Mishkát, bk. i. chap. v.
† *Vide* Article on Janaza or Burial.

The Devil is said to be a fallen angel who was turned out of Paradise because he refused to do homage to Adam.* He is called *Iblís*, a word which is most probably derived from *balas*, a wicked or profligate person; and also *Shaitán* (Satan). Besides angels and devils, there are said to be a distinct order of creatures called *Jinn* (Genii) who were created of fire some thousands of years before Adam. According to tradition the species consists of five distinct orders:—1. *Jánn*; 2. *Jinn*; 3. *Shaitán*; 4. *'Ifrít*; 5. *Márid*.

Their chief abode is the mountains of Qáf, which are supposed to encircle the world.

There are good and evil Genii. If good, they are exceedingly handsome; if evil, they are horribly hideous. The evil genii are said to have been at liberty to enter any of the seven heavens till the birth of Jesus, when they were excluded from three of them. On the birth of Muhammad they were forbidden the other four heavens. They continue, however, to ascend to the confines of the lowest heavens, and there listen to the conversations of the

---

* Surat-ul-Baqr (ii.), 33.

angels respecting the decrees of God, which they sometimes impart to men by means of talismans and invocations.

The good genii are Muslims, and perform all the religious duties of the faithful.

King Solomon is said to have had great power over the genii by means of his magic ring.*

Students of Islam must bear in mind that most of the absurd stories of the genii are related in the Qurán, and have, therefore, received from Muhammad all the authority of a divine revelation.

---

* The second Targum on Esther i.—ii., mentions the four classes of Genii which were given into the power of King Solomon.

XII.—PROPHETS.

The number of prophets (*rasúl*), which have been sent by God, are said to be 224,000, or, according to another tradition, 124,000. Of these 313 were Apostles sent with special commissions, to reclaim the world from infidelity and superstition.

Six brought new laws which successively abrogated the preceding and have special titles, or *kalima* * :—

1. *Adam* (Adam), *Sufi-Ullah*, the Chosen of God.
2. *Nuh* (Noah), *Nabi-Ullah*, the Preacher of God.

---

* Dr. Pfander, in the second chapter of Mizán-ul-Haqq, states that Muhammadan Doctors assert that by the descent of the *Psalms* the Torah was abrogated. Such, however, is *not* the case, for the Psalms are not said to have abrogated the Torah, and consequently David has no special title or *Kalima*.

3. *Ibrahím* (Abraham), *Khalíl-Ullah*, the Friend of God.

4. *Musá* (Moses), *Kalím-Ullah*, one who conversed with God.

5. *'Isa* (Jesus), *Ruh-Ullah*, the Spirit of God.

6. Muhammad, *Rusúl-Ullah*, the Messenger of God.

The number of sacred books delivered to man are said to have been one hundred and four, viz.:—

  Ten, to Adam;
  Fifty, to Seth (*Sísh*);
  Thirty, to Enoch (*Edrís*);
  Ten, to Abraham;
  The Taurát, to Moses;
  The Zabur, to David;
  The Injíl, to Jesus;
  The Qurán, to Muhammad.

The one hundred scriptures given to Adam, Seth, Enoch, and Abraham, are termed *Sahífah* (a pamphlet), and the other four, *Kitáb* (a book); but all that is necessary for the Muslim to know of these books is supposed to have been retained in the Qurán.

Luqmán-i-Hakím (supposed to have been

Æsop) and Alexander the Great are also considered by Muhammadan commentators to have been prophets. Luqmán is mentioned in the thirty-first Sura of the Qurán, and Zulqurnain, "the two-horned" (supposed to have been Alexander), in the eighteenth Sura; but it is not clear as to what position the author of the Qurán intended to assign to these worthies.

Muhammad's enumeration of the Old Testament Prophets, both as to name and chronological order, is exceedingly confused.

XIII. — THE DAY OF RESURRECTION AND JUDGMENT, AND THE SIGNS OF THE LAST DAYS.

Qɪ'ᴀ'ᴍᴀᴛ (lit. "standing"), or the day of resurrection and judgment, is a time which all Muhammadans allow is a perfect secret and known only to God. But they say that the approach of the day of judgment will be known by twenty-five signs.*

1. The decay of faith among men.
2. The advancing of the meanest persons to dignity.
3. That a maid-servant shall become the mother of her mistress.
4. Tumults and seditions.
5. A war with the Turks.
6. Great distress in the world.
7. That the provinces of 'Iráq and Syria shall refuse to pay tribute.

---

* *See* Mishkát-u'-Musábih, bk. xxiii. chap. iii.

8. That the buildings of Medina shall extend to Yaháb.

9. The sun rising in the west.

10. The appearance of a remarkable Beast, called the *Dábbat-ul-arz*, which shall rise out of the earth in the temple at Mecca.

11. War with the Greeks and the taking of Constantinople by 70,000 of the posterity of Isaac.

12. The coming of *Masíh-ud-Dajjál*, or Antichrist.

13. The coming of Jesus Christ, who will descend upon one of the minarets of the Mosque at Damascus.

14. War with the Jews.

15. The ravages made by *Yajúj* and *Majúj* (Gog and Magog).

16. A smoke which shall fill the whole earth.

17. An eclipse of the moon.

18. The return of the Arabians to idolatry.

19. The discovery of a heap of treasure by the retreating of the river Euphrates.

20. The demolition of the temple at Mecca.

21. The speaking of beasts and inanimate things.

22. A breaking out of a fire in Yaman.

23. The appearance of a remarkable man who shall drive men before him with his staff.

24. The coming of Imám Mahdí,* the director, who will come from Khorásán, his troops bearing black ensigns.

25. A mighty wind which shall sweep away the souls of all who have but a grain of faith in their hearts.

The following is a succinct account of the day of judgment, translated from a Muhammadan book:—"Then shall God bring all men back and raise them again, and restore to them their souls, and gather them together. He will then call for the books in which have been written the good and evil actions of all men. Then he will judge them in equity and weigh the balance (*mízán*) of their works, and will make retribution to every soul according to what he has done. Some shall enter Paradise through his goodness and mercy, and some shall go to hell. No *Muslim* shall remain in

---

* Imám Mahdí is said by the Shia'hs to have been their twelfth Imám, Abu Kásim; but who will come again in the last days.

hell for ever, but shall enter into Paradise, after they have suffered according to their sins, for believers shall remain for ever in Paradise, and the unbelievers in hell fire."

Sírát is a bridge which all must pass over on the day of judgment. It is said to extend over the midst of hell, and to be sharper than the edge of a sword. In passing it the feet of the infidel will slip, and he will fall into hell fire; but the feet of the Muslim will be firm, and carry him safely to Paradise.

XIV.—HEAVEN.

THE Muhammadan Paradise is called *Jannat* (garden) in Arabic, and *Bahisht* in Persian; the word *Firdaus*, from which we get our English word Paradise, being restricted to one region in the celestial abodes of bliss.

There are eight different terms employed in the Qurán for heaven, and although they would appear to be but different names for the same region, Muhammadan divines understand them to mean different stages of glory.

They are as follows * :—

1. *Jannat-ul-Khuld* (Sura xxv. 16), "The garden of eternity."
2. *Dár-us-Salám* (Sura vi. 127), "The dwelling of peace."

---

* These various stages of Paradise are variously given by European authors. Those in the text are from the Arabic dictionary, the Ghyás-ul-Loghat, and have been compared with the verses given from the Qurán.

3. *Dár-ul-Qarár* (Sura xl. 42), " The dwelling which abideth."

4. *Jannat-i-'Adan* (Sura ix. 72), " The garden of Eden."

5. *Jannat-ul-Mawá* (Sura xxxii. 19), " The garden of refuge."

6. *Jannat-un-N'aím* (Sura vi. 70), " The garden of delight."

7. *Jannat-i-'Illiyún* (Sura lxxxiii. 18), " The garden of 'Illiyun."

8. *Jannat-ul-Firdaus* (Sura xviii. 107), " The garden of Paradise."

These eight stages of Paradise are spoken of as "*eight doors*" in the Traditions (Mishkát, bk. ii. chap. i.).

The sensual delights of Muhammad's Paradise are proverbial, and they must have exercised considerable influence upon the minds of the people to whom he made known his mission. The allusions in the Qurán are far too numerous to admit of quotation, but they will be found more particularly in Suras lxxvi., lv., lvi., xlvii.

The descriptions of the celestial regions and the enjoyments promised to "the faithful" are still more minutely given in the traditional sayings of the Prophet (Mishkát, bk. xxiii. chap. xiii.).

Apologists for Islám, Carlyle for example, have suggested that the sensual delights of Muhammad's Paradise may after all be taken figuratively, even as the Song of Solomon and the Revelation of St. John. It is quite true that such is the interpretation hinted at in the Akhláq-i-Jaláli; and Mr. Lane in his "Modern Egyptians" says he met a Muslim of learning who considered them figurative; but such is not the view of any Muhammadan commentator. All Muslim theologians have given a literal interpretation of the sensual delights, and it is impossible for any candid mind to read the Qurán and Traditions and arrive to any other conclusion on the subject.

Islám, true to its anti-Christian character, preaches a sensual abode of bliss in opposition to the express teaching of our blessed Lord, who said, "They neither marry nor are given in marriage, but are as the angels of heaven (St. Matt. xxii. 30).

It is remarkable that with the exception of one passage (Sura iii. 25), Muhammad's descriptions of the sensual paradise belong to the later period of his mission, and after he had become a polygamist.

In addition to the seven divisions of celestial bliss, there are said to be seven firmaments (*asmán*).

1. Of pure virgin silver, which is Adam's residence.
2. Of pure gold, which is Enoch's and John Baptist's.
3. Of pearls, which is Joseph's.
4. Of white gold, which is Jesus'.
5. Of silver, which is Aaron's.
6. Of ruby and garnet, which is Moses'.
7. Of crystal, which is Abraham's.

Muhammadans undoubtedly get their tradition of seven heavens from the Talmud; but the Jewish tradition with reference to the seven heavens was a more sensible arrangement than that of the Muhammadans.

The seven heavens of the Jews are as follow * :—

1. The vellum, or curtain.
2. The expanse, or firmament.
3. The clouds of ether.
4. The habitation, where the temple of Jeru-

---

* *See* Dr. Adam Clark on 2 Cor. xii. 2.

salem and the altar are situated, and where Michael the great prince offers sacrifice.

5. The dwelling place, where troops of angels sing.

6. The fixed residence, where are the treasures of snow and hail.

7. Araboth, or special place of glory.

XV.—HELL.

HELL, or the place of torment, is called in Arabic *Jahannam*, and in Persian *Dozakh*; and is said to have seven portals or divisions,* which the Commentator Baghawi distributes as follows :—

1. *Jahannam*, for Muhammadans; for, according to the Qurán, all Muslims will pass through hell.†

2. *Lazwá,* a blazing fire for Christians (Sura lxx. 15 only).

3. *Hutama,* an intense fire for Jews (Sura civ. 4 only).

---

* Sura xv. 44. "It hath seven portals, and at each portal a separate band;" a tradition founded on the Talmud. Thus in Sota 10, David is said to have rescued Absalom from the seven dwellings of hell. (Rodwell.)

† Sura xix. 44, "Verily there is not one of you that shall not go down into hell. *Jahannam* is the Arabic form of the Greek γεέννα, and it is remarkable that the word should be used for a purgatorial hell and not ἄδης which, according to the Papists, denotes that state.

4. *S'aír*, a flaming fire for Sabians (Sura iv. 11, and fourteen other places).

5. *Saqar*, a scorching heat for Magi (Suras liv. 58, and lxxiv. 43).

6. *Jahím*, a huge hot fire for idolaters (Sura ii. 113, and twenty other places).

7. *Háwía*, the bottomless pit for hypocrites (Sura, cl. 8).

The situation of hell is a matter of dispute.

Baghawi's distribution of the different sections of hell is a proof of the utter recklessness of Muslim Commentators, for in neither case are *Lazwá* and *Hutama* apportioned to Christians or Jews in the Qurán.

XVI.—THE DECREES OF GOD.

Taqdi'r, or the absolute decree and predestination of both good and evil, is the sixth article of the Muslim's creed. The orthodox belief is that whatever hath or shall come to pass in this world, whether it be good or bad, proceedeth entirely from the divine will, and is irrevocably fixed and recorded in the *preserved tablet* (*Lahw-ul-Mahfúz*).*

Of this doctrine Muhammad makes great use in his Qurán, and all those who have had any practical acquaintance with the lives of Muhammadans, know well to what extent it influences the daily life of every Muslim. It

---

* *Lahw - ul - Mahfúz*, occurs only once in the Qurán, namely, Sura lxxxv. 22, where it relates to the Qurán being written thereon. The Preserved Tablet on which the actions of men are written, is called *Imám-ul-Mubín*, the clear prototype, Sura xxxvi. 11.

is not only urged as a source of consolation in every trial, but as a palliation of every crime. "It was written in my *taqdír*" (fate), is an excuse familiar to every European who has had much intercourse with Muslim servants or soldiers.

The following is a translation of an Arabic treatise on the subject: " Faith in the decrees of God, is that we believe in our heart and confess with our tongue that the most High God hath decreed all things so that nothing can happen in the world, whether it respects the conditions and operations of things, or good and evil, or obedience and disobedience, or faith and infidelity, or sickness and health, or riches and poverty, or life and death, that is not contained in the written tablet of the decrees of God. But God hath so decreed good works, obedience, and faith, that He ordains and wills them, and that they may be under His decree, His salutary direction, His good pleasure and command. On the contrary, God hath decreed, and does ordain and determine evil, disobedience, and infidelity; yet without His salutary direction, good pleasure and command, but being only by way of seduction, indignation, and prohibition. But whosoever shall say that God is not delighted with good faith, or that God hath not an indignation against evil and unbelief, he is certainly an infidel."

XVII. — THE FIVE FOUNDATIONS OF PRACTICAL RELIGION.

THE five pillars, or foundations, of practice in Islám are :—
1. The recital of the Creed, or *Kalimah*,*—" There is no deity but God, and Muhammad is the Prophet of God."
2. *Sulát.*—The five stated periods of prayer.
3. *Roza.*—The thirty days fast of Ramazán.
4. *Zakát.*—The legal alms.
5. *Hajj.*—The pilgrimage to Mecca.

---

* The enumeration of the *Creed* amongst the foundations of *practice* seems to perplex English writers, and consequently Dr. Macbride (p. 134), and other authors, omit it entirely, and reduce the foundations of practical religion to four. Our readers will observe, however, that it is the *recital* of the creed, and not the creed itself, which forms one of the five practical duties of the Muslim (*vide* next article).

XVIII.—THE RECITAL OF THE CREED.

THE Recital of the *Kalimah*, or Creed, is the first of the five foundations, or pillars of practice, in Islám. It consists of the following sentence, which is always recited in Arabic:—

Lá-iláha-il-lal-laho Muhammad-ur-Rasúl-Ullah, "There is no deity but God, and Muhammad is the Apostle of God."*

When any one is converted to Islám he is required to repeat this formula, and the following are the conditions required of every Muslim with reference to it:—

1.—That it shall be repeated aloud, at least once in a life-time.

---

* We have here translated *rasúl*, "Apostle," although it is generally rendered "Prophet," which, however, is the more correct rendering of *nabí*, a word which also occurs in the Qurán. Both *nabí* and *rasúl* are translated into Persian and Hindustani by *paighambar*, which is translated into English by either Prophet, Apostle, or Mes-

2.—That the meaning of it shall be fully understood.

3.—That it shall be believed in "by the heart."

4.—That it shall be professed until death.

5.—That it shall be recited correctly.

6.—That it shall be always professed and declared without hesitation.

Something similar to this celebrated symbol of the Muhammadan creed appears to have existed in Arabia previous to the foundation of Islamism. Dr. Arnold in his work on "Islám and Christianity," quotes the following prayer from the writings of Abulfaraj, which is said to have been used by the idolatrous Arabians :—" I dedicate myself to Thy service, O God! Thou hast no companion, except Thy companion, of whom Thou art absolute Master of whatever is his." *

---

* Circumcision (*Khatnah*) although never once enjoined in either the Qurán or Traditions, is an institution of Islám; but it is not incumbent upon adults, the recital of the creed being sufficient.

XIX.—PRAYER.

PRAYER (Arabic *Sulát*, Persian and Hindustani *Namáz*, Pushto *Nmuz*) is the second of the five foundations of practice in Islám. The constant round of devotion which characterizes Muhammadan nations is a very remarkable phenomenon in the system. We translate the words *Sulát* and *Namáz* by the English word *prayer*, although this "second foundation" of the religion of Muhammad is something quite distinct from that prayer which the Christian poet so well describes as the "soul's sincere desire uttered or unexpressed." It would be more correct to speak of the Muhammadan *Namáz* as a *service*; "prayer" being more correctly rendered by the Arabic *du'a*. In Islám prayer is reduced to a mechanical act, as distinct from a mental act; and in judging of the spiritual character of Muhammadanism, we must take into careful consideration the precise character of that devotional service which every Muslim is required to render to God at least *five* times a day,* and which, undoubtedly, exercises so great an influence upon the character of the followers of Muhammad.

It is absolutely necessary that the service should be performed in Arabic; and that the clothes and body of the worshipper should be clean, and that the praying place should be free from all impurity. It may be said either privately, or in company, or in a Mosque—although services in a Mosque are more meritorious than those elsewhere.

It is always preceded by ablution *(Wuzu),*† and, if said in a Mosque, by the *Azán* and

---

* It is remarkable that there is but one passage in the Qurán in which the stated times of prayer are enjoined, and that it mentions only *four* and not five periods :— Surat-ur-Rum (xxx.), 17, "Glorify God when it is evening (*masa*), and at morning (*subh*),—and to Him be praise in the heavens and in the earth,—and at afternoon ('*ashí*), and at noon-tide (*zuhr*)." But all commentators are agreed that *masa* includes both sun-set and after sunset; and, therefore, both the *Maghrib* and '*Ishaa* prayers.

† *Wuzu* is the ablution of the face, hands, feet, &c., which is necessary before every time of prayer. *Ghusal*, or the washing of the whole body, is performed after certain legal defilements.

Iqámat, terms which will be explained afterwards.

The regular form of prayer begins with the *Niyyat*, which is said standing, with the hands on either side :—

"I have purposed to offer up to God only, with a sincere heart this morning (or, as the case may be), with my face Qibla-wards, two (or, as the case may be) *rak'at* prayers *Farz* (*Sunnat*, or *Nafl*)."

Then follows the Takbír-i-Tahrímah, said with the thumbs touching the lobules of the ears and the open hands on each side of the face :—

"God is great!"

The Qíám, or standing position. The right hand placed upon the left, below the navel,* and the eyes looking to the ground in self-abasement. During which is said the Subhán †:—

"Holiness to Thee, O God!"
"And praise be to Thee!"
"Great is Thy name!"

---

* The Shafia', and the two other orthodox sects, place their hands on their breasts; as also the Wahhábis. The Shía'hs keep their hands on either side. In all the sects the women perform the Qíám with their hands on their breasts.

† The Shía'hs omit the Subhán.

"Great is Thy greatness!"

"There is no deity but Thee!"

The T'auuz * is then said as follows:—

"I seek refuge from God from cursed Satan."

After which the Tasmíyah is repeated:—

"In the name of God, the compassionate, the merciful."

Then follows the Fátihah, *viz.*, the first chapter of the Qurán †:—

"Praise be to God, Lord of all the worlds!"

"The compassionate, the merciful!"

"King on the day of reckoning!"

"Thee only do we worship, and to Thee only do we cry for help."

"Guide Thou us in the straight path,"

"The path of those to whom Thou hast been gracious;"

"With whom Thou art not angry,"

"And who go not astray."—Amen.

After this the worshipper can repeat as many chapters of the Qurán as he may wish; he should, at least, recite one long or two short verses. The following chapter is

---

* The T'auuz is also called the *'Aúzobillah.*

† The recital of the Qurán is called the *Qira'at,* or reading.

usually recited, namely, the Surat-ul-Ikhlás, or the 112th chapter:—

"Say: He is God alone:"
"God the Eternal!"
"He begetteth not,"
"And is not begotten;"
"And there is none like unto Him."

The Takbír-i-Ruku', said whilst making an inclination of the head and body and placing the hands upon the knees, separating the fingers a little.

"God is great!"

The Tasbih-i-Ruku', said in the same posture.

"I extol the holiness of my Lord, the Great!"*

"I extol the holiness of my Lord, the Great!"

"I extol the holiness of my Lord, the Great!"

The Qiám-i-Sami Ullah or Tasmía', said with the body erect, but, unlike the former Qiám, the hands being placed on either side. The Imám says † aloud,

"God hears him who praises Him."

---

* The Shía'hs here add, "and with his praise." This is also added by the Shía'hs to the Tasbíh-i-Sijdah.

† When the prayers are said by a person alone he recites both sentences.

The people then respond in a low voice.

"O Lord, Thou art praised."

Takbír-i-Sijdah, said as the worshipper drops on his knees.

"God is great!"

Tasbíh-i-Sijdah, recited as the worshipper puts first his nose and then his forehead to the ground.

"I extol the holiness of my Lord, the most High!"

"I extol the holiness of my Lord, the most High!"

"I extol the holiness of my Lord, the most High!"

Then raising his head and body and sinking backward upon his heels, and placing his hands upon his thighs, he says the Takbír-i-Jalsa.*

"God is great!"

Then, whilst prostrating as before, he says the Takbír-i-Sijdah.

"God is great!"

And then during the prostration the Tasbíh-i-Sijdah as before.

"I extol the holiness of my Lord, the most High!"

---

* The Shía'hs here omit the Takbír, and say instead, "I rise and sit by the power of God!"

"I extol the holiness of my Lord, the most High!"

"I extol the holiness of my Lord, the most High!"

Then, if at the close of one rak'at, he repeats the Takbír standing, when it is called Takbír-i-Qiám; but at the end of two rak'ats, and at the close of the prayer, he repeats it sitting, when it is called Takbír-i-Qa'úd.*

"God is great!"

Here ends one rak'at or form of prayer. The next rak'at begins with the Fátihah or 1st chapter of the Qurán. At the close of every two rak'ats he recites the Attahíyat, which is said whilst kneeling upon the ground. His left foot bent under him he sits upon it, and places his hands upon his knees and says † :—

"The adorations of the tongue are for God, and also the adorations of the body, and alms-giving!"

"Peace be on thee, O Prophet, with the mercy of God and His blessing!"

"Peace be upon us and upon God's righteous servants!"

---

* The Shía'hs here recite the Takbír:—"God is great!" with the thumbs touching the lobules of the ear, and add, "I seek forgiveness from God, my Lord, and I repent before Him!"

† The Shía'hs omit the Attahíyat.

Then raising the first finger of the right hand he recites the Tashahhúd:—

"I testify that there is no deity but God*; and I testify that Muhammad is the servant of God, and the messenger of God!" †

The Darúd is said whilst in the same posture.

"O God, have mercy on Muhammad and on his descendants, ‡ as Thou didst have mercy on Abraham and on his descendants. Thou art to be praised, and Thou art great. O God, bless Muhammad and his descendants, as Thou didst bless Abraham and his descendants!"

"Thou art to be praised, and Thou art great!"

Then the Du'a—

"O God our Lord, give us the blessings of this life, and also the blessings of life everlasting. Save us from the torments of fire."§

---

* The Shía'hs add, "who has no partner."
† Every two rak'ats close with the Tashahhúd.
‡ The Shía'hs merely recite:—"God have mercy on Muhammad and his descendants;" and omit the rest.
§ The Du'a is omitted by the Shía'hs, who recite the following instead:—"Peace be on thee, O Prophet, with the mercy of God and His blessing!" "Peace be upon us, and upon God's righteous servants!"

He then closes with the Salám.

Turning the head round to the right, he says—

"The peace and mercy of God be with you."

Turning the head round to the left, he says—

"The peace and mercy of God be with you."

At the close of the whole set of prayers, that is, of Farz, Sunnat, Nafl, or Witr, the worshipper raises his hands * and offers up a "*Munáját*," or supplication. This usually consists of prayers selected from the Qurán or Hadís. They ought to be said in Arabic, although they are frequently offered up in the vernacular.

These daily prayers are either *Farz, Sunnat, Nafl,* or *Witr. Farz,* are those number of rak'ats, (or forms of prayer,) said to be enjoined by God. *Sunnat* those founded on the practice of Muhammad. *Nafl,* the voluntary performance of two rak'ats, or more, which may be omitted without sin. *Witr,* an odd number

---

* The hands are raised in order to catch a blessing from heaven, and they are afterwards drawn over the face in order to transfer it to every part of the body.

of rak'ats, either one, three, five or seven, said after the night prayer. These divisions of prayer are entirely distinct from each other. They each begin afresh with the *Niyyat*. The worshippers may rest for awhile between them, but not converse on worldly subjects. The Wahhábis think it correct to say the *Sunnat* prayers in their houses and only the *Farz* prayers in the mosque.*

In order that our readers may be able to judge of the mechanism of this Muhammadan performance of prayer, we annex a time-table of the Muslim's common prayer, showing the number of *rak'ats* or forms; from which it will be seen what is required of a pious Muhammadan. The five times of prayer are enjoined in the Qurán, the other three periods of prayer are voluntary. (*See* next page.)

Upon reference to the form of prayer, or rak'ats, which we have given, and which admits

---

* Mr. Palgrave, in his "Central and Eastern Arabia," states that he observed that the Wahhábis were careless as to the legal ablutions. Perhaps he was not aware that the worshippers had performed the ablutions, and had said the *Sunnat* rak'ats privately before they came into the mosque.

114 PRAYER.

No.	Time.	Arabic.	Persian.	Hindustani.	Pushto.	Sunnat which are optional.	Sunnat before Farz.	Farz.	Sunnat after Farz.	Nafl.	Witr.
					THE NAMES FOR THE TIME OF PRAYER.			THE NUMBER OF RAK'ATS SAID.			
1	From dawn to sun-rise.	Sulát-ul-Fajr.	Namáz-i-Subh.	Fajr-kí-Namáz.	da-Sahár-nmuz.	...	2	2	...	...	...
2	When the sun has begun to decline.	Sulát-ul-Zuhr.	Namáz-i-Peshín.	Zohar-kí-Namáz.	da-Máspe-khín-nmuz.	...	4	4	2	2	...
3	Mid-way between No. 2 and No. 4.	Sulát-ul-'Asar.	Namáz-i-Dígar.	'Asur-kí-Namáz.	da-Mázi-ger-nmuz.	4	...	4	...	...	...
4	A few minutes after sun-set.	Sulát-ul-Maghrib.	Namáz-i-Shám.	Maghrib-kí-Namáz.	da-Mákh-ám-nmuz.	...	...	3	2	2	...
5	When the night has closed in.	Sulát-ul-'Ishae.	Namáz-i-Khuftan.	'Aysha-kí-Namáz.	da-Maz-khuftan-nmuz.	4	...	4	2	2	7
1	When the sun has well risen.	Sulát-ul-Ishráq.	Namáz-i-Ishráq.	Ishráq-kí-Namáz.	da-Ishráq-nmuz.	...	...	...	...	8	...
2	About 11 o'clock A.M.	Sulát-ul-Zuha.	Namáz-i-Chást.	Zoha-kí-Namáz.	da-Ghar-mí-nmuz.	...	...	...	...	8	...
3	After mid-night	Sulát-ul-Tahajud.	Namáz-i-Tahajud.	Tahajud-kí-Namáz.	da-Shpe-nmuz.	...	...	...	...	9	...

THE FIVE PERIODS OF PRAYER. (Nos. 1–5)

THREE PERIODS WHICH ARE VOLUNTARY. (Nos. 1–3)

of no change or variation, whether used for the "time of travelling," in the "time of danger," or in the "time of need," it will be seen that notwithstanding the beauty of its devotional language, it is simply a superstitious rite, having nothing in common with the Christian idea of prayer.

The devotions of Islám are essentially "vain repetitions," for they must be said in the Arabic language, and admit of no change or variety. The effect of such a constant round of devotional forms, which are but the service of the lips, on the vast majority of Muhammadans, can be easily imagined. We believe that the absence of anything like *true* devotion from these services accounts for the fact that religion and true piety stand so far apart in the practice of Islám.

In addition to the daily prayers, the following are special services for special occasions:

Sulát-ul-Juma'.—" The Friday Prayer." It consists of two rak'ats after the daily meridian prayer.

Sulát-ul-Musáfir.—" Prayers for a traveller."

Two rak'ats instead of the usual number at the meridian, afternoon, and night prayers.

Sulát-ul-Khauf.—"The prayers of fear." Said in time of war. They are two rak'ats recited first by one regiment or company and then by the other.

Sulát-ul-Taráwih.—Twenty rak'ats recited every evening during the Ramazán, immediately after the fifth daily prayer.

Sulát-ul-Istikhára.—Prayers for success or guidance. The person who is about to undertake any special business, performs two rak'at prayers and then goes to sleep. During his slumbers he may expect to have "*ilhám,*" or inspiration, as to the undertaking for which he seeks guidance!

Sulát-ul-Khasúf.—Two rak'ats said at the time of an eclipse of the moon.

Sulát-ul-Kusúf.—Two rak'ats said at the time of an eclipse of the sun.

The *Azán*, is the summons to prayer proclaimed by the *Muazzin*, or crier, in small mosques from the door or side, but in large mosques it ought to be given from the minaret (*manárat*). The following is a translation,

"God is great! God is great! God is great! God is great! I bear witness that there is no God but God! (repeated twice) I bear witness that Muhammad is the Apostle of God! (repeated twice) Come to prayers! Come to prayers! Come to salvation! Come to salvation!* God is great! There is no other God but God!" †

In the early morning the following sentence is added: "Prayers are better than sleep."

The summons to prayer was, at first, the simple cry, " Come to prayer." Bingham tells us that a similar custom existed at Jerusalem (*vide* Antiquities, vol. ii. p. 489) : " In the monastery of virgins which Paula, the famous Roman lady, set up, and governed at Jerusalem, the signal was given by one going about and singing *halleluja*, for that was their call to church, as St. Jerome informs us."

The *Iqámat* (lit. " causing to stand ") is a recitation at the commencement of prayers in a congregation, after the worshippers have taken

---

* The Shía'hs add, " Come to good works !"
† The Shía'hs recite the last sentence twice.

up their position. It is exactly the same as the *Azán*, with the addition of the words, "prayers are now ready."

The Iqámat of the Shafia' and the Wahhábis is just half the length of that of the Hanifis.

XX.—RAMAZA'N, OR THE MONTH OF FASTING.

THE *Ramazán* * is the ninth month of the Muhammadan year, which is observed as a strict fast from the dawn of day to sunset of each day in the month. The excellence of this month was much extolled by Muhammad, who said that during Ramazán " the gates of Paradise are open, and the gates of hell are shut, and the devils are chained by the leg "; and that "only those who observe it will be permitted to enter by the gate of heaven called *Rayyán.*" Those who keep the fast " will be pardoned all their past venial sins."† In the

---

* The word *Ramazán* is derived from *Ramz*, to burn. The month is said to have been so called either because it used (before the change of the calendar) to occur in the hot season, or because the month's fast is supposed to burn away the sins of men. (See *Ghyás-ul-Loghát.*)

† Mishkát-ul-Musábih, bk. vii. chap. i. sect. 1.

month of Ramazán, Muhammad said, the Qurán began to be revealed from heaven.*

The fast does not commence until some Musalman is able to state that he has seen the new moon. If the sky be over-clouded and the moon cannot be seen, the fast begins upon the completion of thirty days from the beginning of the previous month.

The Ramazán must be kept by every Musalman, except the sick, the infirm, and pregnant women, or women who are nursing their children. Young children, who have not reached the age of puberty, are exempt, and also travellers on a journey. In the case of a sick person or a traveller, the month's fast must be kept as soon as they are able to perform it. This is called *Qazá*, or expiation.

The fast is extremely rigorous and mortifying, and when the Ramazán happens to fall in the summer and the days are long, the prohibition even to drink a drop of water to slake the thirst is a very great hardship. Muhammad speaks of this religious exercise as "easy,"† as most probably it was when com-

---

* Qurán, Surat-i-Baqr, verse 181.
† *Ibid.*

pared with the ascetic spirit of the times. Sir William Muir * thinks Muhammad did not foresee that, when he changed the Jewish intercalary year for the lunar year, that the fast would become a grievous burden instead of an easy one; but Muhammadan lexicographers say, the fast was established when the month occurred in the hot season (*see* note, p. 119).

During the month of Rámazán twenty additional *rak'ats*, or forms of prayer, are repeated after the night prayer. These are called *Taráwíh*.

Devout Muslims seclude themselves for some time in the Mosque during this month, and abstain from all worldly conversation and engage themselves in the reading of the Qurán. This seclusion is called '*Itiqáf*. Muhammad is said to have usually observed this custom for the last ten days of Ramazán.

The *Laylut-ul-Qadr*, or the "night of power," is said by Muhammad to be either on the twenty-first, twenty-third, or twenty-fifth, or twenty-seventh, or twenty-ninth. The exact date of this solemn night has not been dis-

---

* Life of Mahomet, iii. p. 49.

covered by any but the Prophet himself, and some of the Companions, although the learned doctors believe it to be on the twenty-seventh. Of this night Muhammad says in the Qurán (Surat-ul-Qadr):—

"Verily we have caused it (the Qurán) to descend on the night of power.

"And who shall teach thee what the night of power is?

"The night of power excelleth a thousand months;

"Therein descend the angels and the spirit by permission

"Of their Lord in every matter;

"And all is peace till the breaking of the morn."

By these verses commentators * understand that on this night the Qurán came down entire in one volume to the lowest heaven, from whence it was revealed by Gabriel in portions as the occasion required. The excellences of this night are said to be innumerable, and it is believed that during it the whole animal and vegetable kingdom bow in humble adoration

---

* Tafsír-i-Hoseini.

to the Almighty, and the waters of the sea become sweet in a moment of time! This night is frequently confounded * with the *Shab-i-Barát*; but even the Qurán itself does not appear to be quite clear on the subject, for in the *Surat-i-Dukhán* we read, " By this clear book. See, on a *blessed night* have we sent it down, for we would warn mankind, on the night wherein all things are disposed in wisdom." In which it appears that the *blessed night*, or the *Laylut-ul-Mubarak*, is both the night of record and the night upon which the Qurán came down from heaven, although the one is supposed to be the twenty-seventh day of Ramazán, and the other the fifteenth of Shabán.

M. Geiger identifies the Ramazán with the fast of the *tenth* (Leviticus xxiii. 27); it is, however, far more likely that the fast of the Tenth is identical with the 'Id-i-Ashura, not only because the Hebrew '*Asúr*, ten, is retained in the title of that Muhammadan fast; but also because there is a Jewish tradition (*vide* Adam Clark), that creation began upon the

---

* By Lane, in his "Egyptians," and by other writers.

Jewish fast of the Tenth, which coincides with the Muhammadan day 'Ashura, being regarded as the day of creation. Moreover, the Jewish 'Asur and the Muslim 'Ashura are both fasts and days of affliction. It is far more probable that Muhammad got his idea of a thirty days' fast from the Christian Lent. The observance of Lent in the Eastern Church was exceedingly strict both with regard to the nights as well as the days of that season of abstinence; but Muhammad entirely relaxed the rules with regard to the night, and from sunset till the dawn of day the Muslim is permitted to indulge in any lawful pleasures and to feast with his friends; consequently large evening dinner-parties are usual in the nights of the Ramazán amongst the better classes. This would be what Muhammad meant when he said, "God would make the fast an ease and not a difficulty," for notwithstanding its rigour in the day-time, it must be an easier observance than the strict fast observed during Lent by the Eastern Christians of Muhammad's day.

XXI.—ZAKA'T, OR LEGAL ALMS-GIVING.

Zaka't (lit. "purification"), the legal alms, or poor rate, is the fourth of the five foundations of practice. Zakát should be given annually of five descriptions of property, provided they have been in possession a whole year; namely, money, cattle, grain, fruit, and merchandise. There are several minor differences amongst the various sects as to the precise explanation of the law with reference to these legal alms; but the following are the general rules observed by Sunni Musulmáns :—

(1.) Money. If he is a *Sáhib-i-Nissáb* (*i. e.* one who has had forty rupees in his possession for a year), he must give alms at the rate of one rupee in every forty, or two and a half per cent.

(2.) Cattle. Should his property consist of sheep or goats, he is not obliged to give alms until they amount to forty in number. He must then give one for one hundred and twenty, and two for the next eighty, and then one for every hundred afterwards. For camels the following is the rate:—from 5 to 24, one sheep or goat; from 25 to 35, one yearling female (*bint-i-mukház*) camel; from 36 to 45, one two-year old female (*bint-i-labún*) camel; from 46 to 60, one three-year old female (*hiqqah*) camel; from 61 to 75, one four-year old female (*jaz'ah*) camel; from 76 to 90, two two-year old female camels; from 91 to 120, two three-year old female camels; and from 121 and upwards, either a two-year old female camel for every forty, or a three-year old female camel for every fifty.

For cows or bulls:—If 30 cows, a one-year old female calf; if 40, a two-year old female calf, and so on, a one-year old female calf for every 10.

Alms for buffaloes are the same as for sheep.

For horses, either the same rate as for camels, or two rupees eight annas for every horse whose value exceeds one hundred rupees. Animals used for riding, and beasts of burden, are exempt.

(3.) Fruits. For fruits watered by rain a tenth is given; but if irrigated, then a twentieth part.

(4.) Grain. The same rate as for fruits.

(5.) Merchandise. For the capital, as well as for the profits, *Zakát* is given at the rate of one in forty, provided the owner be a Sáhib-i-nissáb. For gold bullion, half a *misqál* ($=67\frac{1}{2}$ grains) is given for every 20 misqál weight. For silver bullion at the rate of $2\frac{1}{2}$ per cent. For whatever is found in mines, if over 240 dirhams in weight ($=$ 2 lbs. 2 oz. 2 dr.), a fifth is required; and if the money be laid out in merchandise, alms are to be given on the profits.

Wood and pearls are exempt, and also clothing; but not jewels.

The following are the classes of persons on whom it is lawful to bestow the Zakát:—

1. Such pilgrims to Mecca as have not the means of defraying the expenses of the journey.

2. Religious mendicants.

3. Debtors who cannot discharge their debts.

4. Beggars.

5. Poor travellers.

6. Proselytes to Muhammadanism.

The *Zakát*, or legal alms, must be distinguished from the *Sadaqa*, or offerings, which is a term more especially applied to the offerings on the '*Id-ul-Fitr* (*q.v.*) although it is used for almsgiving in general.

As far as we have been able to ascertain, it does not appear that the Muhammadans of the present day are very regular in the payment of the Zakát, which ought to be given on the termination of a year's possession. In countries under Muhammadan rule it is exacted by Government.

It is somewhat remarkable that Muhammad in his institution of legal almsgiving did not more closely copy the Jewish law in the giving of the "tenths," more particularly as the number ten appears to have been so frequently preferred as a number of selection in the cases of offerings in both sacred and secular history. The Muhammadan *Zakát*, however, differs very materially from the Jewish tithe; for the latter was given to the Levites of the Temple, and employed by them for their own support and for that of the priests, as well as for festival purposes. The Muhammadan priesthood are supported by grants of land,* and offerings at the time of harvest, and are not permitted to take any of the *Zakát*. Moreover, the descendants of the "Prophet" are not allowed to accept of either *Zakát* or *Sadaqa*, because "they are of the Prophet's own blood and not to be included in the indigent."

Whatever may be the weak points in Muhammadanism, all candid observers, acquainted with the condition of Muhammadan nations, must admit that its provision for the poor is highly commendable. As we have journeyed from village to village amongst the Afghans, we have been frequently struck with the absence of great poverty; and even in our large cities, where Muhammadan beggars are numerous, it must be remembered that they are either religious mendicants or professional beggars, and for the most part quite unworthy of charitable relief.

---

* Land, or any property appropriated for religious or charitable purposes, is called *waqaf*.

XXII.—HAJJ, OR PILGRIMAGE TO MECCA.*

HAJJ, or Pilgrimage to Mecca, is the fifth of the five foundations of practice. It is said, by Muhammad, to be of Divine institution, and has the authority of the Qurán for its observance.† Its performance is incumbent upon those men and women who have sufficient means to meet the expenses of the journey,

---

* Only three Englishmen are known to have visited Mecca, and to have witnessed the ceremonies of the Pilgrimage:—Joseph Pitts, of Exeter, A.D. 1678; John Lewis Burckhardt, A.D. 1814; Lieut. Richard Burton, of the Bombay Army, A.D. 1853. The narratives of each of these "pilgrims" have been published. The first account in English of the visit of a European to Mecca, is that of Lodovico Bartema, a gentleman of Rome, who visited Mecca in 1503. His narrative was published in Willes and Eden's Decades, A.D. 1555.

† *Vide* Qurán, Sura xxii. 28.

and to maintain their families at home during their absence.

The ceremonies observed on this occasion are so ridiculous that they do more to reveal the imposture of Muhammad than any other part of his system. They are, even by the confession of Muhammadans themselves, the relicts of the idolatrous superstitions of ancient Arabia; and they are either evidences of the dark and superstitious character of Muhammad's mind, or, what is perhaps even more probable, they show how far the "Prophet" found it suit his purpose to compromise with the heathen Arabians of his day. The merits of the pilgrimage are so great, that every step taken in the direction of the *K'aba* blots out a sin; and he who dies on his way to Mecca is enrolled on the list of martyrs.

However ingeniously the apologists of Islám may offer excuses for some of the weak points of Muhammad's religious system, and endeavour to shield the "Prophet of Arabia" from the grave and solemn charge of having "forged the name of God," the pilgrimage to Mecca can admit of no satisfactory solution. In its institution the false prophet layeth open his own folly, for in the ridiculous ceremonies of the Hajj, we see the law-giver, whose professed mission it was to uproot the idolatry of Arabia, giving one of its superstitious customs the authority of a Divine enactment. The pilgrimage to Mecca is one of the numerous inconsistencies of Muhammad's pretended revelation.

The following is the orthodox way of performing the pilgrimage, founded upon the example of the "Prophet" himself.

Upon the pilgrim's arrival at the last stage* near Mecca, he bathes himself, and performs two rak'at prayers, and then divesting himself of his clothes, he assumes the pilgrim's sacred robe, which is called *Ihrám*. This garment consists of two seamless wrappers, one being wrapped round the waist, and the other thrown loosely over the shoulder, the head being left uncovered. Sandals may also be worn, but not shoes or boots. After he has assumed the pilgrim's garb, he must not anoint his head, shave any part of his body, pare his nails, nor

---

* These are six in number, and are situated about five or six miles from Mecca in different directions. They are called *Miqát*.

wear any other garment than the *Ihrám*. Immediately on his arrival at Mecca he performs the legal ablutions, and proceeds to the *Musjid-ul-Harám*, or Sacred Mosque, and kisses the *Hajr-ul-aswad*, or the black stone, and then encompasses the *K'aba** seven times. This act, which is called *Tawáf*, is performed by commencing on the right and leaving the *K'aba* on the left. The circuits are made thrice with a quick step or run, and four times at a slow pace.† He then proceeds to the *Maqám-i-Ibrahím* (the place of the prophet Abraham) and performs two *rak'at* prayers, after which he returns to the black stone and kisses it. He then goes to the gate of the temple leading to Mount Safá, and from it ascends the hill and

---

* Some confusion exists in the minds of English authors with regard to the word *K'aba*. The Temple or Mosque at Mecca is called Musjid-ul-Harám (the sacred Mosque), or Bait-ullah (the house of God). The *K'aba* (lit. a cube) is the square stone building in the centre, containing the black stone. And the Hajr-ul-aswad is the black stone itself, which Muslims say was originally white, but became black by reason of men's sins.

† Sharastani informs us, that there was an opinion prevalent amongst the Arabs that the walking round the K'aba, and other ceremonies, were symbolic of the motion of the planets, and of other astronomical facts. (*Rodwell*.)

runs from the summit of Mount Safá to that of Mount Marwah seven times! On the top of the hill he remains for a few moments, and raising his hands heavenwards supplicates the Almighty.

On the eighth day, which is called *Tarwíah*, he unites with his fellow-pilgrims at Miná in the usual services of the Muslim ritual, and stays the night.

After morning prayer he rushes to Mount 'Arifát, where, having said two rak'at prayers with the Imám and heard the *Khútbah* (or oration), he remains until sunset. He then proceeds to Muzdalífah, and having said the sunset and night prayers, he stays the night at that place.

The next morning, which is the *'Id-ul-Azhá*, or great feast, he comes to three places in Miná, marked by three pillars called *Jamra*. At each of these pillars he picks up seven small stones, or pebbles, and having said some particular prayer over each pebble and blown upon it, he throws it at one of the pillars. This ceremony is called *Rami-ul-Jamár*, or the throwing of pebbles.

He then proceeds to the place of sacrifice at

Miná, and performs the usual sacrifice of the 'Id-ul-Azhá; after this sacrifice he gets himself shaved, and his nails pared. The pilgrim garb is then removed and the pilgrimage is ended, although he should rest at Mecca the three following days, which are called the *Ayyám-ut-Tashríq*, or the days of drying up the blood of the sacrifice. These are three days of well earned rest after the vigorous peripatetic performances of the last four days.

The pilgrimage must be performed on three days of the month of *Zul Hijja*, namely from the seventh to the tenth; a visit to Mecca at any other time has not the merit of a pilgrimage.

Before he leaves Mecca the pilgrim should once more perform the circuits round the *K'aba*, and throw stones at the sacred pillars, each seven times.

He then proceeds to Medina, and makes his salutations at the Shrine of Muhammad. The Walhábis do not perform the last act, as it is contrary to their principles to visit shrines.

The Musulmán who has performed the pilgrimage is called *Hájí*.

The *K'aba* is also called the *Qibla*, or the

direction to which Muslims are to pray. Mosques are, therefore, always erected Qibla-wards. At the commencement of Islám, the Qibla was Jerusalem; but when Muhammad failed to conciliate the Jews to his prophetic pretensions, he made the *K'aba* the *Qibla*, or the direction in which to pray.

The pilgrimage cannot be performed by proxy, as some English authors have stated, although it is considered a meritorious act to pay the expenses of one who cannot afford to perform it. But if a Muhammadan on his death-bed bequeath a sum of money to be paid to a certain person to perform the pilgrimage, it is considered to satisfy the claims of the Muslim law. If a Muslim have the means of performing the pilgrimage, and omit to do so, its omission is equal to a *kabíra*, or mortal sin.

XXIII.—THE LAW.

MUHAMMADAN law consists of two divisions, *Rawá* and *Nárawá*, *i. e.*, Things lawful and Things unlawful.

I.—That which is lawful is divided into five classes.

1. *Farz.*—That which has been enjoined in the Qurán.

2. *Wájib.*—That of which there is some doubt as to its Divine institution.

3. *Sunnat.*—The example of Muhammad, which consists of three kinds :—

> *Sunnat-i-F'ilí.*—That which Muhammad himself did.
>
> *Sunnat-i-Qaulí.*—That which Muhammad said should be practised.
>
> *Sunnat-i-Taqrírí.*—That which was done in the presence of Muhammad and which he did not forbid.

4. *Mustahab.* — That which Muhammad sometimes did and sometimes omitted.

5. *Mubáh.* — That which may be left unperformed without any fear of Divine punishment.

II.—Things unlawful are of three classes :—

1. *Harám.* — That which is distinctly forbidden in the Qurán and Hadís.

2. *Makrúh.* — That of which there is some doubt as to its unlawfulness, but which is generally held to be unclean or unlawful.

3. *Mufsid.* — That which is corrupting and pernicious.

The divisions of lawful and unlawful *do not merely apply to food*, but also to ablutions and other customs and precepts.

XXIV.—SIN.

THE Muhammadan doctors divide sins into two classes, very much as the Roman Catholic divines do; the usual Roman designation being that of *mortal* and *venial sin*, whilst Muhammadans use the expressions *Kabíra* and *Saghíra*, " Great " and " Little." *Kabíra* are those great sins, of which, if a Musalman do not repent, he will go to the purgatorial hell reserved for sinful Muslims. The divines of Islám are not agreed amongst themselves as to the exact number of Kabíra sins, but they are generally considered to be seventeen (*vide* Fawáid-us-Shari'at).

1. *Kufr*, or infidelity.
2. Constantly committing *Saghíra*, or little sins.
3. Despairing of the mercy of God.
4. Considering one's self safe from the wrath of God.

5. False witness.

6. *Qazaf*, or falsely charging a Musulman with adultery.

7. Taking a false oath.

8. Magic.

9. Drinking wine.

10. Appropriation of the property of orphans.

11. Usury.

12. Adultery.

13 Unnatural crimes.

14. Theft.

15. Murder.

16. Fleeing in battle before the face of an infidel.

17. Disobedience to parents.

XXV.—PUNISHMENT.

PUNISHMENT is divided into three classes :— *Hadd, T'azír,* and *Qisás.*

1. *Hadd* is that punishment which is said to have been ordained of God in the Qurán and the Hadís, and which must be inflicted. The following belong to this class :—*Adultery,* for which the adulterer is stoned. *Fornication,* for which one hundred stripes are inflicted. *Drunkenness,* for which there are eighty stripes. The *slander of a married person,* that is, bringing a false charge of adultery against a married person, for which the offender must receive eighty lashes. This punishment is said to have been instituted by God, when 'A'yesha, the favourite wife of "the Prophet," was falsely charged with adultery! *Apostacy,* for which the *Murtadd,* or Apostate, is killed, unless he repent of his error within three days. When an Apostate from Islám has been killed according to the law, or has left the country,

his property goes to those of his heirs who still remain *Musulmáns* (*vide* the "Al Sirajiyah").

2. *T'azír* is that punishment which is said to have been ordained of God, but of which there are not special injunctions, the exact punishment being left to the discretion of the Qází, or Judge.

3. *Qisás* (lit. "retaliation") is that punishment which can be remitted by the person offended against, upon the payment of a fine or compensation. The punishment for murder is of this class. The next akin to the murdered person can either take the life of his kinsman's murderer, or accept a money compensation (*Díat*). There is also retaliation in case of wounds. Qisás is the *lex talionis* of Moses, "eye for eye, tooth for tooth, hand for hand, foot for foot, burning for burning, wound for wound, stripe for stripe" (*vide* Exodus xxi. 24). But in allowing a money compensation for murder, Muhammad departed from the Jewish code.

XXVI.—LAWFUL FOOD.

No animal is lawful food unless it be slaughtered according to the Muhammadan law, namely, by drawing the knife across the throat and cutting the windpipe, the carotid arteries, and the gullet, repeating at the same time the words "*Bismillah Allaho Akbar,*" *i. e.* "In the name of the great God." A *clean* animal, so slaughtered, becomes lawful food for Muslims, whether slaughtered by Jews, Christians, or Muhammadans.

In the "Sharah Waqaia" it is said that the following creatures are lawful (*halál*) :—

1. Those animals that are cloven-footed and chew the cud, and are not beasts of prey.

2. Birds that do *not* seize their prey with their claws, or wound them with their bills, but pick up food with their bills.

3. Fish; but no other animals which move in the water.

4. Locusts.

Some commentators say that the horse is lawful; but it is generally held to be "*makrúh*."

Fish found dead in the water is unlawful; but if it be taken out and die afterwards it is lawful.

Alligators, turtles, crabs, snakes, frogs, etc., are unlawful. Wine is expressly forbidden in the Qurán; and, in the judgment of the learned, this prohibition extends to whatever has a tendency to intoxicate, such as opium, bhang, chars,* and tobacco. The Akhund of Swat † has issued several "*fatwáhs*," prohibiting the use of tobacco; but the chilam (or pipe), having become a national institution, no notice has been taken of the inhibition. The Wahhábis do not permit its use. In Trans-Indus territory, the hukka, or chilam, is never allowed in a mosque.

---

* Bhang and Chars are intoxicating preparations of hemp.

† The Akhund of Swát is a great religious leader amongst the Muhammadans of North India and Central Asia. He resides at Seydú, in Swát, about twenty miles beyond the British frontier.

From what we have written, it will be seen that a Muslim can have no religious scruples to eat with a Christian, as long as the food eaten is of a lawful kind. Sayyid Ahmad Khán Bahádur, C.S.I., has written a treatise proving that Muhammadans can eat with the *Ahl-i-Kitáb*, namely, Jews or Christians. The Muhammadans of India, whilst they will eat food cooked by idolatrous Hindus, refuse to touch that cooked either by Native or European Christians; and they often refuse to allow Christians to draw water from the public wells, although Hindus are permitted to do so. Such objections arise solely from jealousy of race, and an unfriendly feeling towards the ruling power. In Afghanistan and Persia, no such objections exist; and no doubt much evil has been caused by Government allowing Hindustani Musulmans to create a religious custom which has no foundation whatever, except that of national hatred to their English conquerors.

XXVII.—FARZ-I-KAFA'I'.

Farz-i-Kafa'i' are those commands which are imperative (*farz*); but which, if one person in eight or ten perform, it is equivalent to all having performed it.

1. To return a salutation.
2. To visit the sick, and inquire after their welfare.
3. To follow a bier on foot to the grave.
4. To accept an invitation.
5. To reply to a sneeze, *e. g.* if a person sneeze, and say immediately afterwards, "God be praised" (*Alhamdo lillah*), it is incumbent upon at least one of the party to exclaim, "God have mercy on you" (*Yarhamuk Allah*).

There is an interesting chapter on the custom of saluting after sneezing in Isaac D'Israeli's "Curiosities of Literature," from which it appears that it is almost universal amongst nations.

XXVIII.—FITRAT.

FITRAT (lit. "nature") is said to be certain ancient practices of the prophets before the time of Muhammad, which have not been forbidden by him.

In the Hadís "*Muslim*," the customs of *fitrat* are said to be ten in number.

1. The clipping of the mustachios, so that they do not enter the mouth.
2. Not cutting or shaving the beard.
3. Cleaning the teeth (*i. e. miswák*).
4. Cleansing the nostrils with water at the usual ablutions.
5. Cutting the nails.
6. Cleaning the finger-joints.
7. Pulling out the hairs under the arms.
8. * * * *
9. * * * *
10. Cleansing the mouth with water at the time of ablution.

XXIX.—SALUTATIONS.

The usual Muhammadan salutation is "*as salámu 'alekam*," *i. e.* "The peace of God be with you."

When a person makes a "*salám*," and any of the assembly rise and return it, it is considered sufficient for the whole company.

The lesser number should always be the first to salute the greater; he who rides should salute him who walks; he who walks, him who stands; the stander, the sitter, etc. A man should not salute a woman on the road; and it is considered very disrespectful to salute with the left hand, that hand being used for legal ablutions.

The ordinary salute is made by raising the right hand either to the breast or to the forehead.

In Central Asia the salutation is generally given without any motion of the hand or body.

Pupils salute their masters by kissing the hand or sleeve, which is the usual salutation made to men of eminent piety.

Homage is paid by kissing the feet of the ruler, or by kissing the ground or carpet.

In Afghanistan, conquered people pay homage by casting their turbans at the feet of the conqueror; and the heads of tribes often lessen the size of their turbans before appearing in the presence of their rulers.

XXX.—THE CALIPH.

The Caliph, or *Khalífa* (*i. e.* the *vicegerent* of the Prophet), is the sovereign dignity amongst Muhammadans, vested with absolute power. The word more frequently used for the office in Muhammadan works of jurisprudence is *Imám* (leader), or *Imám-ul-'Azam* (the great leader). It is held to be an essential principle in the establishment of the office, that there shall be only one Caliph at the same time; for the Prophet said:—" When two Caliphs have been set up, put the last to death and preserve the second, for the last is a rebel" (*vide* Mishkát, bk. xvi. chap. i.). According to all Sunní Muhammadan books, it is absolutely necessary that the Caliph be "a man, an adult, a sane person, a free man, a learned divine, a powerful ruler, a just person, and one of the Quraish" (*i. e.* of the tribe to which the Prophet himself belonged). The Shía'hs, of course, hold that he should be one of the descendants of the Prophet's own family; but this is rejected by the Sunnis and Wahhábis. The condition that the Caliph should be of the Quraish, is very important; for thereby the present Ottoman Sultans fail to establish their claims to the Caliphate.

After the deaths of the first five Caliphs,— Abu Bakr, Omar, Osmán, Ali, and Hasan,— the Calıphate, which is allowed by all parties to be *elective*, and not hereditary, passed successively to the Ommiades and Abbasides. The temporal power of the Abbaside Caliphs was overthrown by Houlakon Khan, son of the celebrated Jengiz Khán, A.D. 1258; but, for three centuries, the descendants of the Abbaside, or Bagdad, Caliphs resided in Egypt, and asserted their claim to the spiritual power.

The founder of the present dynasty of Ottoman Sultans was Osman, the son of a tribe of Ogıouz Turks, a powerful chief, whose descendant, Bazazet I., is said to have obtained the title of *Sultán* from one of the Abbaside Caliphs in Egypt, A.D. 1389. When Selim I. conquered Egypt (A.D. 1516), it is asserted that he obtained a transfer of the title of Caliph to himself from one of the successors of the old Bagdád Caliphs. It is, however, a mere assertion; for the title and office being elective, and not hereditary, it was not in the power of any Caliph to transfer it to another. Force of circumstances alone has compelled the ruler of the Ottoman Empire to assume the position, and has induced his subjects to acquiesce in the usurpation. We have not seen a single work of authority, nor met with a single man of learning, who has ever attempted to prove that the Sultans of Turkey are rightful Caliphs; for the assumption of the title by any one who is not of the Quraish tribe is undoubtedly illegal and heretical, as will be seen from the following authorities:—

(*Mishkát-ul-Musábih*, bk. xxiv. chap. xii.)

"Ibn-i-Umr relates that the Prophet of God said:—' The Caliphs shall be in the Quraish tribe as long as there are two persons in it, one to rule and another to serve.'"

(*Sharh-ul-Muwáqif*, p. 606. Arabic Edition. Egypt.)

"It is a condition that the Caliph (*Imám*) be of the Quraish tribe. All admit this, except the Khawárij and certain Mutazilahs. We all say with the Prophet: 'Let the Caliph be of the Quraish'; and it is certain that the Companions acted upon this injunction, for Abu Bakr urged it as an authority upon the Ansárs, on the day of Sakhifah, when the Companions were present and agreed. It is, therefore, for a certainty established that the Caliph must be of the Quraish."

(The *Hujjat-Ullah-al-Bálaghah*, p. 335. Arabic Edition. Delhi.)

"It is a necessary condition that the Caliph (*Imám*) be of the Quraish tribe."

(The *Kashháf-i-Istaláhat*. A Dictionary of Technical Terms. Edited by Colonel N. Lees, *in loco*.)

"The Caliph (*Imám*) must be a Quraish."

It is a matter of history that the Wahhábis regarded the Turkish Sultan as a usurper when Sana took Mecca and Medina in 1804; and to the present day, in countries not under Turkish rule, the Khutbah is recited in behalf of the Amír, or ruler of the Muslim state, instead of the Ottoman Sultan, which would not be the case if he were acknowledged as a lawful Caliph. In a collection of Khutbahs, entitled the *Majmua' Khutbah*, the name of the Sultan does not once occur, although this collection is much used in Muhammadan states. We have seen it stated that the Sultan is prayed for in Hyderabad and Bengal; but, we believe, it will be found, upon careful inquiry, that he was not mentioned *by name*, until very recently, in any of the mosques of India. Khutbah in which there are prayers for the Ottoman Sultan by name, have been imported from Constantinople; but, whoever may be the rightful Caliph, it is certain that, according to law, the only sovereign who can be prayed for in an Indian mosque, is " Alexandrina Victoria, Empress of India " (*Qaisar-i-Hind*); for all Muhammadans admit that the Friday Khutbah cannot be recited without the permission of the ruler.

XXXI.— MUHAMMADAN CLERGY, SCHOLARS, AND SAINTS.

THE Muslims have no hereditary priestly caste as the Hindus, nor have they a distinct order of clergy exactly corresponding with those of the Christian Church. But still there is a powerful hierarchy possessed of great political and religious influence, which resembles the Jewish Scribes and Lawyers.

In countries under Muhammadan rule the religious dignitaries are appointed by the king, who is properly the highest spiritual authority in the kingdom. The Shekh-ul-Islám at Constantinople unites in himself the functions of the Primate and Lord Chancellor.

The following are the chief religious functionaries, in a state governed according to Muhammadan law.

Qází.—The minister of justice, who passes

sentence in all cases of law; religious, moral, civil, or criminal.

Muftí.—The law officer, who expounds the law, and in difficult cases supplies the *Qází* with "*fatwás*" or decisions.

There are still persons in India bearing the titles of *Qází* and *Muftí*, but the offices have ceased to exist under British Government. The Indian law, however, permits *civil* cases being decided by Muhammadan divines, if both parties consent to the arrangement.

Imám.—The Arabic word *Imám* is said, by Sale, to answer to the Latin *antistes*, the president of the temple. It is also used for the four successors of Muhammad, the four great doctors of the four orthodox sects, the twelve great leaders of the Shía'hs, and for any great religious leader. It is, however, commonly used for the person who leads the daily prayer, and is in receipt of the revenues of the mosque.

The titles of *Qází, Muftí,* and *Imám* may be said to embrace the various appointments held by Muhammadan divines; but there are also numerous titles to denote doctors of Science and Divinity.

Tabíb. A doctor of medicine.

Hakím. A doctor of philosophy, used also for a doctor of medicine.

Muhaqqiq. A very learned doctor in one or two sciences.

Maulawí, also *Mullá.* A doctor of divinity, used for any person who has been educated in the Muhammadan religion, and assumes the office of teacher.

Faqíh. A doctor of law.

Mutakallim. A doctor of theology.

Muhaddis. A doctor of the law of the traditions.

Mufassir. One learned in the commentaries on the Qurán.

Madarrís. An academical doctor, *i. e.*, one educated in some school of reputation.

Doctors of Divinity are of three grades: *Maulaví*, *'Alim* (pl. *'Ulama*), *Mujtahid* (pl. *Mujtahidín*). The title of *Mujtahid* is held by very few Sunní Muhammadans, but is more common amongst the Shía'hs.

In addition to these titles, which express the degree of learning, there are others which denote the piety and sanctity of the individual. *Pír* and *Walí* are the common titles; but the following express certain degrees of reputed sanctity:—

'A'bid, one constantly engaged in the worship of God.

Záhid, one who leads a life of asceticism. The title of *Faqír* does not always denote one who has renounced the possessions of the world, but is applied to any one of a humble spirit, one poor in the sight of God, rather than in need of worldly assistance.

Qutbah and *Ghaus*, the highest orders of sanctity. According to vulgar tradition, a Ghaus is a saint whose ardour of devotion is such, that in the act of worship his head and limbs fall asunder! whilst a *Qutbah* is one who is supposed to have attained to the state of sanctity which reflects the heart of the Prophet.

There are four titles of respect which scarcely belong to either the religious or the learned class, but are of more general use:—

Shekh, an appellation which literally signifies an elder or aged person. It is a common title of respect, and is almost synonymous with our English "*Mister*." In Egypt and Arabia it appears to be used for the Hindustani and Persian *Khán*, or chief.

Miyán, (lit. "a master" or "friend") generally used for the descendants of celebrated saints, but also as a title of respect.

Sayyid, generally pronounced *Syud* (lit. "lord"). For the descendants of Muhammad from his daughter Fatimah and her husband 'Ali. The word Sayyid is often used as part of a name, without reference to family descent from the Prophet; as Sayyid Ahmad, Sayyid Shah, &c.

Mír, also used for Sayyids, but not exclusively.

XXXII.—THEOLOGICAL LITERATURE.

MUHAMMADAN theological literature is very extensive, and in consequence of the cheapness of lithographic printing, it is daily increasing.

The following are its chief divisions :—

(1.) *Hadís*.—Accounts of the precepts and practice of Muhammad. The collectors of Hadís may be numbered by hundreds, but the chief authorities are the six books known as the *Siháh-i-Sita*, or "*six correct books.*" The popular work on the subject amongst the Sunnis of India being the Mishkát-ul-Musábih. (*See* article on Traditions.)

(2.) *Usúl* (lit. "roots ").—Treatises on the rules and principles of the four foundations of the Islám law,—being expositions of the exegesis of the Qurán and Hadís, and the principles of Ijma' and Qiás. The most popular works on this subject are the Manár, by

Abdullah ibn Ahmad, A.H. 710, and the *Talwi' Tauzia'*, by 'Ubaid-Ullah ibn Mas'ud, A.H. 747.

(3.) *'Aqáid* (lit. " creeds ").—Expositions of scholastic theology, founded upon the six articles of faith. The most celebrated exposition of the Islám creed being that by Imám Ghazáli, A.H. 505. In India the work most read is the *Sharah-i-'Aqáid*, by Maulaví Mas'ud S'ad-ud-dín Taftazáni, A.H. 792.

(4.) *Fiqah*.—Works on Muhammadan law, whether civil or religious. The work most read amongst Sunnis is the *Hidáyah*, written by a learned man named 'Ali, A.H. 593; part of which has been translated by the late Colonel Charles Hamilton. A smaller work, entitled the *Sharah Waqaiah*, by Abdul Haqq, is also much used.

(5.) *Tafsír*.—Commentaries on the Qurán. These are very numerous, and contain very many Jewish traditions of the most worthless character. One of the latest and most learned of these productions is said to be the short commentary by Shah Wali Ullah of Delhi, who died A.H. 1176.

The best known commentaries amongst the Sunnis are Baizáwi (A.H. 685), Madárik (A.H.

701), Jalálain (A.H. 911), Baghawi (A.H. 515), Mazhári (A.H. 1225), *Hoseini* (A.H. 900).

(6.) *Siyar*.—Ecclesiastical history, *i. e.* the history of Muhammad and his successors. This branch of literature, Sayyid Ahmad Khan of Aligarh says, "is the one which requires the most emendation."

The chief authorities on the life of Muhammad and early days of Islám, in addition to the Hadís, are Ibn Isháq, Ibn Hishám, Wáqidi, and Tabarí; whilst the most popular histories amongst the Sunnis of India are the Rawzat-ul-Ahbáb, by 'Ataa Ullah ibn Fazl Ullah, A.H. 1000, and the Madárij-un-Nabuwat, by Shekh Abdul Haqq, A.H. 1025.

In addition to his theological studies, the Muhammadan student is instructed in *Mantiq* (logic), *Sarf* (inflexion), and *Nahw* (syntax).

The text of a book is called *Matan*, the marginal notes *Hashíyah*, and its commentary *Sharh*.

XXXIII.—MUHARRAM AND 'A'SHURA'A

THE *Muharram* (lit. "that which is sacred") commences on the first of the month * of that name, and is continued for ten days, the tenth day being called *'A'shuráa*. They are days of *mátam*, or lamentation, in commemoration of the martyrdom of 'Ali, and of Hasan,

---

* The twelve months of the Muhammad lunar year are as follows :—

1. Muharram.	The sacred month.
2. Safar.	The month which is void.
3. Rabí'-ul-awwal.	The first of spring.
4. Rabi'-ul-ákhir.	The last of spring.
5. Jamád-al-úlá.	The first dry month.
6. Jamád-al-ukhrá.	The last of spring.
7. Rajab.	The revered month.
8. Sh'abán.	The month of division.
9. Ramazán.	The hot month.
10. Shawwál.	The month for going forth (hunting).
11. Zul-Q'ada.	The month of rest.
12. Zul-Hijja.	The month of pilgrimage.

and Husain,* as observed by the Shía'hs; but the day *'A'shuráa* (the tenth) is also held sacred by the Sunnís, the observance of the month having been enjoined by Muhammad on account of its having been the month of creation.

The ceremonies of the Muharram differ much in different places; but the following are the main features of the festival as observed by the Shía'hs. A place is prepared which is called the *'A'shúr-khána* (the ten-day house), or *Imám-Bára* (the Imám place), in the centre of which is dug a pit, in which fires are kindled, and at night the people, young and old, fence across the fire with sticks and swords, and whilst dancing round it, call out, "Oh 'Ali! noble Hasan! noble Husain! bridegroom! alas friend! stay! stay! etc.; the cry being repeated in the most excited manner hundreds of times, until the whole assembly has reached the highest pitch of excitement. They then form

---

* The Khalífa 'Ali was assassinated in the Mosque of Cufa, A.D. 660. Hasan was poisoned by his wife, at the instigation of Yazíd. Husain was slain, with three and thirty strokes of lances and swords, A.D. 680. The story of Husain is one of the most touching pages of Muslim history.

themselves in circles, and beat themselves with chains in the most frantic manner. The women repeat a funeral eulogium, and the Maulavís, the *Rowzat-us-Shuhádáa,* or the Book of Martyrs.

On the seventh day there are representations of the marriage ceremony of Qásim, and of the martyrdom of Husain; and on the eighth day a lance or spear is carried about the city to represent Husain's head, which was carried on the point of a javelin by order of Yazíd. In addition to these representations, there are the Tázías, Tábúts, or biers, of the tombs of Hasan and Husain, a horse-shoe in representation of Husain's swift horse, and the standards of Hasan, Husain, and Qásim, and other Muslim celebrities.

The Sunní Muhammadans do not usually take part in these ceremonies, but observe the tenth day, *'A'shuráa,* being the day on which God is said to have created Adam and Eve, heaven, hell, the tablet of decree, the pen, fate, life, and death.

Muhammad commanded his followers to observe the *'A'shuráa* by bathing, wearing new clothes, applying *surma* * to the eyes, fasting, prayers, making peace with one's enemies, associating with religious persons, relieving orphans, and giving of alms.

The fast of *'A'shurác* is a *Sunnat fast*, *i. e. not* founded upon an injunction in the Qurán, but upon the example of Muhammad.

---

* Surma is antimony or galena ground to a fine powder, and applied to the eyelids to improve the brightness of the eyes.

XXXIV.—A'KHIRI CHAHA'R SHAMBA.*

A'KHIRI CHAHA'R SHAMBA is the "*last Wednesday*" of the month of Safar, and is a feast held in commemoration of Muhammad's having experienced some mitigation of his last illness and having bathed. It was the last time he performed the legal bathing, for he died on the twelfth day of the next month. In some parts of Islám it is customary, in the early morning of this day, to write seven verses of the Qurán, known as the *Seven Salàms*, and then wash off the ink and drink it as a charm against evil.

The A'khiri Chahár Shamba is not observed by the Wahhábís, not being enjoined in the Qurán and Hadís.

---

* The Persian name for the day; the Arabic being *Arb'áa-ul-Akhír*, *i. e.* "the last Wednesday."

XXXV.—BA'RA WAFA'T.*

THE *Bára Wafát* (*i. e. Bára*, "twelve," and *Wafát*, "death") is the twelfth day of the month, Rabí-ul-Awwal. It is observed in commemoration of Muhammad's death.

On this day, *Fátihahs* (*i. e.* the first chapter of the Qurán), are said for Muhammad; and both in private houses and in the mosques, the learned recite portions of the Traditions and other works in praise of the excellences of Muhammad. These customs are usually observed for the whole twelve days, although the twelfth day is held most sacred.

The Wahhábís do not observe the *Bára Wafát*, as its observance is not enjoined in the Qurán or Hadís.

---

* The Hindustani name of the day, there being no special title for the day in Persian or Arabic.

XXXVI.—SHAB-I-BARA'T.*

SHAB-I-BARA'T, the "night of record," is observed on the fifteenth day of the month, Sh'abán. It is the "Guy Fawkes Day" of India, being the night for display of fireworks.

On this night, Muhammad said, God registers annually all the actions of mankind which they are to perform during the year; and that all the children of men, who are to be born and to die in the year, are recorded. Muhammad enjoined his followers to keep awake the whole night, to repeat one hundred *rak'at* prayers, and to fast the next day; but there are generally great rejoicings instead of a fast, and large sums of money are spent in fireworks. The Shab-i-Barát must not be confounded with

---

* The Persian title; the Arabic being *Laylat-ul-Mubaraka*.

the *Laylat-ul-Qadr* (night of power), mentioned in the Qurán, which is the twenty-seventh night of the Ramazán. The *Shab-i-Barát*, however, is frequently called *Shab Qadr*, or the night of power, by the common people.

XXXVII.—'ID-UL-FITR, OR THE LESSER FESTIVAL.

'ID-UL-FITR (lit. "the feast of breaking the fast"), is called also the feast of Ramazán, the Feast of Alms, and the Minor Festival. It is held on the first day of the month of Shawwál, which is the day after the close of the Ramazán fast. On this day, before going to the place of prayer, the *Sadaqa*, or propitiatory offerings, are made to the poor in the name of God. The offerings having been made, the people assemble either in the Jama'-i-Masjid (*i. e.* the principal mosque), or proceed to the *'Idgah*, which is a special place for worship on festivals. The worship commences with two *rak'at* prayers, after which the Imám takes his place on the second step of the *mimbar* (pulpit) and recites the *Khutbah*, concluding with a prayer for the king. After this is ended, he offers up a *munáját*, or supplication, for the people, for the remission of sins, the recovery of the sick, increase of rain, abundance of corn, preservation from misfortune, and freedom from debt. He then descends to the ground, and makes further supplication for the people, the congregation saying *Amín* at the end of each supplication. At the close of the service the members of the congregation salute and embrace each other, and offer mutual congratulations, and then return to their homes, and spend the rest of the day in feasting and merriment.

XXXVIII.—'ID-UL-AZHA', OR THE FEAST OF SACRIFICE.

ID-UL-AZHA,* or the Feast of Sacrifice, is called also *Yaum-un-Nahr, Qurbán-i-'Id, Qurbán Bayrám, Baqr-i-'Id* (the Cow Festival), and the Great Feast, and is held on the tenth day of the month Zul-Hijja. This festival has become part of the Meccan pilgrimage, of which it is the concluding scene, although it appears that Muhammad at first intended to conform to the custom of the Jews in observing the great day of atonement, but, when he failed to maintain a friendly footing with the Jews, he merged the rite into the Meccan pilgrimage. This feast, however, is the great Muhammadan festival, which is observed wherever Islám exists; and it is a notable fact that whilst Muhammad professed to abrogate the Jewish

---

* Vulg. *'Id-uz-Zohá.*

ritual, and also ignored entirely the doctrine of the atonement as taught in the New Testament, denying even the very fact of our Saviour's crucifixion, he made the "*day of sacrifice*" the great central festival of his religion.

There is a very remarkable Hadís, related by 'A'yesha, who states, that Muhammad said, "Man hath not done anything on the 'Id-ul-Azhá more pleasing to God than spilling blood; for verily the animal sacrificed will come, on the day of resurrection, with its horns, its hair, and its hoofs, and will make the scales of his (good) actions heavy. Verily its blood reacheth the acceptance of God, before it falleth upon the ground, therefore be joyful in it."* Muhammad has thus become unwillingly a witness to the grand doctrine of the Christian faith that "without shedding of blood, there is no remission." The animal sacrificed must be without blemish, and of full age; but it may be either a goat, a sheep, a cow, or a camel.

According to the commentator Jalál-ud-dín Syúty, the sacrifice was instituted in com-

---

* Mishkát-ul-Masábih, bk. iv. chap. xlii. sect. 2.

memoration of Abraham's willingness to sacrifice his son *Ismaíl*! The following is the account given by Muhammadan writers:—"When Ibrahím (the peace of God be upon him) founded Mecca, the Lord desired him to prepare a feast for Him. Upon Ibrahím's (the friend of God) requesting to know what He would have on the occasion, the Lord replied, 'Offer up thy son Ismaíl.' Agreeably to God's command he took Ismaíl to the K'aba to sacrifice him, and having laid him down, he made several ineffectual strokes on his throat with a knife, on which Ismaíl observed, 'Your eyes being uncovered, it is through pity and compassion for me you allow the knife to miss: it would be better if you blindfolded yourself with the end of your turban and then sacrificed me.' Ibrahím acted upon his son's suggestion and having repeated the words '*bismillah allah-ho akbar*' (*i.e.*, 'in the name of the great God'), he drew the knife across his son's neck. In the meanwhile, however, Gabriel had substituted a broad-tailed sheep for the youth Ismaíl, and Ibrahím unfolding his eyes observed, to his surprise, the sheep slain, and his son standing behind him." The account is a ridiculous parody upon the words of the inspired prophet Moses. In the Qurán the name of the son is not given, although commentators state, that the Prophet said, that he was a descendant of the son of Abraham who was offered in sacrifice.* The sacrifice, as it is now performed on the 'Id-ul-Azhá is as follows:—The people assemble for prayer at the 'Idgah as on the 'Id-ul-Fitr; after prayers the people return to their houses. The head of the family then takes a sheep (or a cow or camel) to the entrance of his house and sacrifices it, by repeating the words, " In the name of the great God," and cutting its throat. The flesh of the animal is then divided, two-thirds being kept by the family, and one-third being given to the poor in the name of God.

---

* The name is not given in the Qurán, but it is in the Hadís Sahíh Bokhári.

XXXIX.—NIKAH, OR MARRIAGE.

NIKAH, is the celebration of the marriage contract as distinguished from the festive rejoicings which usually accompany it; the latter being called *Shádí* in Persian and Urdú, and *'Urs* in Arabic.

Marriage, according to Muhammadan law, is simply a *civil* contract, and its validity does not depend upon any religious ceremony.

The legality of marriage depends upon the consent of the parties, which is called *I'jáb* and *Qabúl*, viz. declaration and acceptance; the presence of two male witnesses, or one male and two females*; and a dower of not less than ten dirhems to be settled upon the woman. The omission of the settlement does not, however, invalidate the contract; for, under any

---

* In Muhammadan law woman, instead of being man's "better half," is only equal to half a man!

circumstances, the woman becomes entitled to her dower of ten dirhems or more. Muhammadans are permitted by the Qurán* to marry four free women, and to have as many female slaves as he may possess. Marriages for a limited period were sanctioned by "the Prophet"; but this law is said to have been abrogated, although it is allowed by the Shía'hs even in the present day. These temporary marriages are called *Mut'ah*, and are undoubtedly the greatest blot in Muhammad's moral legislation.

Marriage is enjoined upon every Muslim, and celibacy is frequently condemned by Muhammad. The "clergy" are all married men, and even the *ascetic* orders are, as George Herbert would have said, "rather married than unmarried." It is related in the Hadís, that Muhammad said that, "when the servant of God marries, he perfects half his religion." Not long ago we met a Faqír of the Nukshbandía order, a man of considerable reputation

---

* "Of women who seem good in your eyes marry two, or three, or four; and if ye fear that ye shall not act equitably, then one only, or the slaves whom ye have acquired." (Sura iv. 3.)

at the court of Cabul, who said that he wished to lead a celibate life, but that his disciples had insisted upon his "perfecting his religion" by entering upon the married state!

As the religious ceremony does not form part of the legal conditions of marriage, there is no uniformity of ritual observed in its celebration. Some Qázís merely recite the *Fátihah* (the first chapter of the Qurán), and the *Darúd*, or blessing; but the following is the more common order of performing the service. The Qází, the bridegroom, and the bride's attorney, with the witnesses having assembled in some convenient place, arrangements are made as to the amount of Dower, or *Mahr*. The bridegroom then repeats after the Qází the following :—

1. The *Istighfár*, "I desire forgiveness from God, who is my Lord."

2. The four chapters of the Qurán commencing with the word "*Qul*." These chapters have nothing in them connected with the subject of marriage, and appear to be selected on account of their brevity.

3. The *Kalima*, or Creed. "There is no deity but God, and Muhammad is the Prophet of God."

4. The *Sift-ul-Imán*. A profession of belief in God, the angels, the scriptures, the prophets, the resurrection, and in fate or absolute decree of good and evil.

The Qází then requests the bride's attorney to take the hand of the bridegroom, and to say, "Such an one's daughter, by the agency of her attorney, and by the testimony of two witnesses, has, in your marriage with her, had such a dower settled upon her, do you consent to it?" To which the bridegroom replies, "With my whole heart and soul, to my marriage with this woman as well as to the dower already settled upon her, I consent, I consent, I consent!"

After this the Qází raises his hands, and offers the following prayer:—

"O great God! grant that mutual love may reign between this couple, as it existed between Adam and Eve, Abraham and Sarah, Joseph and Zulekha,* Moses and Zipporah, his Highness Muhammad and 'A'yesha, and his Highness 'Ali Murtuza and Fátimah-uz-Zahra."

---

* According to Muhammad, Joseph afterwards married Zulekha, the widow of Potiphar.

The ceremony being over, the bridegroom embraces his friends and receives their congratulations. Nikah is preceded and followed by festive rejoicings, which have been variously described by Oriental travellers; but they are not parts of either the civil or religious ceremony.

XL.—TALA'Q, OR DIVORCE.

In Islám the wife is the property of the husband, and consequently she can be disposed of by divorce at a moment's notice. The law has, however, placed certain slight restrictions upon the exercise of this right, and has ruled that there are three kinds of divorce :—

(1.) *Taláq-i-Ahsan*, or "the *most laudable* form of divorce," is when the husband divorces his wife when she is in a state of purity, by one sentence, "*thou art divorced*," or words to that effect. This is esteemed the best form, because the sentence having been only pronounced *once*, the husband can again change his mind, with the consent of his divorced wife, at any subsequent period, until she marries another.

(2.) *Taláq-i-Hasan*, or " a *laudable* form of divorce," is when the husband divorces his wife by prououncing the sentence, "*thou art divorced*," during his wife's period of purity, and at intervals of a month.

(4.) *Taláq-i-Bid'aí*, or "an *irregular* form of divorce," is when the husband repeats the sentence three times on one occasion.

Whenever the sentence of divorce is repeated three times it is a *Taláq-i-Mutlaq*, or an irrevocable divorce, after which the husband cannot marry his repudiated wife until she has married and lived with another, and is divorced by her second husband.

In all cases of repudiation, except when a wife requests her husband to divorce her, the dower must be repaid to the woman, an arrangement which often prevents a man exercising the privilege.

The ground of divorce, under the Mosaic law, was "some uncleanness in her" (*vide* Deut. xxiv. 1—4), and of which there were two well-known interpretations. The school of Shammai seemed to limit it to a moral delinquency in the woman, whilst that of Hillel extended it to the most trifling causes. Our Lord appears to have confirmed the interpretation of Shammai (St. Matt. v. 32), whilst Muhammad adopted that of Hillel, but dispensing with the "bill of divorcement" enjoined by the Mosaic code, thereby placing the woman entirely at the will and caprice of her husband.

XLI.—JANA'ZA, OR BURIAL.

JANA'ZA is the term used both for the bier and for the Muhammadan funeral service. The burial service is founded upon the practice of Muhammad, and varies but little in different countries, although the ceremonies connected with the funeral procession are diversified. In Egypt, for instance, the male relations and friends of the deceased precede the corpse, whilst the female mourners follow behind. In North India and Central Asia, women do not usually attend funerals, and the friends and relatives of the deceased walk behind the bier. There is a tradition amongst some Muhammadans that no one should precede the corpse, as the angels go before. Funeral processions in Central Asia are usually very simple in their arrangements, and are said to be more in accordance with the practice of the "Prophet," than those of Egypt and Turkey. It is considered a very meritorious act to carry the bier, and four from among the near relations, every now and then relieved by an equal number, carry it on their shoulders. Unlike our Christian custom of walking slowly to the grave, Muhammadans carry their dead quickly to the place of interment; for Muhammad is related to have said, that it is good to carry the dead quickly to the grave to cause the righteous person to arrive soon at happiness, and if he be a bad man it is well to put wickedness away from one's shoulders. Funerals should always be attended on foot; for it is said, that Muhammad on one occasion rebuked his people for following a bier on horseback. "Have you no shame?" said he, "since God's angels go on foot, and you go upon the backs of quadrupeds?" It is a highly meritorious act to attend a funeral, whether it be that of a Muslim, a Jew, or a Christian. There are, however, two traditions given by Bokhárí, which appear to mark a change of feeling on the part of the time-serving Prophet of Arabia towards the Jews and Christians. "A bier passed by the Prophet, and he stood up; and it was said to the Prophet, this is the bier of a Jew. 'It is the holder of a soul,' he replied, 'from which we should take warning and fear.'" This rule is said to have been abrogated, for, "on one occasion the Prophet sitting on the road when a bier passed, and the Prophet disliked that the bier of a Jew should be higher than his head, and he therefore stood up." Notwithstanding these contradictory traditions, we believe that in all countries Muhammadans are wont to pay great respect to the funerals of both Jews and Christians. Not long ago, about sixty Muhammadans attended the funeral of an Armenian Christian lady at Peshawur, when the funeral service was read by the Native clergyman. In the procession the Muhammadans took their turn with the Native Christian converts in carrying the bier, and assisting in lowering the coffin into the grave. During the reading of the service, some few seated themselves on the grass, but the majority listened attentively to the funeral office, which was impressively read by the Native pastor, himself a Christian convert from Muhammadanism.

The Muhammadan funeral service is not recited in the graveyard, it being too polluted a place for so sacred an office; but either in a mosque, or in some open space near the dwelling of the deceased person, or the graveyard. The owner of the corpse, *i. e.* the nearest relative, is the proper person to recite the service; but it is usually said by the family Imám, or the village Qází.

The following is the order of the service:—

Some one present calls out,—

"Here begin the prayers for the dead."

Then those present arrange themselves in three, five, or seven rows opposite the corpse, with their faces Qiblawards (*i. e.* towards Mecca). The Imám stands in front of the ranks opposite the head* of the corpse, if it be that of a male, or the waist, if it be that of a female.

The whole company having taken up the *Qiám*, or standing position, the Imám recites the Niyat.

"I purpose to perform prayers to God, for this dead person, consisting of four *Takbírs*."

Then placing his hands to the lobes of his ears, he says the first *Takbír*.

"God is great!"

Then folding his hands, the right hand placed upon the left, below the navel, he recites the *Subhán*:—

"Holiness to Thee, O God,"
"And to Thee be praise."

---

* The Shía'hs stand opposite the loins of a man.

"Great is Thy Name."

"Great is Thy Greatness."

"Great is Thy Praise."*

"There is no deity but Thee."

Then follows the second *Takbír*:—

"God is great!"

Then the *Darúd*:—

"O God, have mercy on Muhammad and upon his descendants, as Thou didst bestow mercy, and peace, and blessing, and compassion, and great kindness upon Abraham and upon his descendants."

"Thou art praised, and Thou art great!"

"O God, bless Muhammad and his descendants, as Thou didst bless and didst have compassion and great kindness upon Abraham and upon his descendants."

Then follows the third *Takbír*:—

"God is great!"

After which the following prayer (*Dua'*) is recited:—

"O God, forgive our living and our dead, and those of us who are present, and those who are absent, and our children, and our full

---

* This sentence is not generally recited in the Subhán of the daily prayer.

grown persons, our men and our women. O God, those whom Thou dost keep alive amongst us, keep alive in Islám, and those whom thou causest to die, let them die in the Faith."

Then follows the fourth *Takbír*:—

"God is great!"

Turning the head round to the right, he says:—

"Peace and mercy be to Thee."

Turning the head round to the left, he says:—

"Peace and mercy be to Thee."

The *Takbír* is recited by the Imám aloud, but the *Subhán*, the *Salám*, the *Darúd*, and the *Dua'*, are recited by the Imám and the people in a low voice.

The people then seat themselves on the ground, and raise their hands in silent prayer in behalf of the deceased's soul, and afterwards addressing the relatives they say, "It is the decree of God." To which the chief mourner replies, "I am pleased with the will of God." He then gives permission to the people to retire by saying, "There is permission to depart."

Those who wish to return to their houses do so at this time, and the rest proceed to the grave. The corpse is then placed on its back in the grave, with the head to the north and feet to the south, the face being turned towards Mecca. The persons who place the corpse in the grave repeat the following sentence : " We commit thee to earth in the name of God and in the religion of the Prophet."

The bands of the shroud having been loosed, the recess, which is called the *láhd*, is closed in with unburnt bricks and the grave filled in with earth. In some countries it is usual to recite the *Súrat i Twá Háh* as the clods of earth are thrown into the grave; but this practice is objected to by the Wahhábís, and by many learned divines. This chapter is as follows :—

" From it (the earth) have We (God) created you, and unto it will We return you, and out of it will We bring you forth the second time."

After the burial, the people offer a *fátihah* (*i.e.*, the first chapter of the *Qurán*) in the name of the deceased, and again when they have proceeded about forty paces from the grave they offer another *fátihah*; for at this juncture, it is said, the two angels Munkar and

Nakír examine the deceased as to his faith.*
After this, food is distributed to beggars and religious mendicants as a propitiatory offering to God, in the name of the deceased person.

If the grave be for the body of a woman, it should be to the height of a man's chest, if for a man, to the height of the waist. At the bottom of the grave the recess is made on the side to receive the corpse, which is called the *láhad*. The dead are seldom interred in coffins, although they are not prohibited.

To build tombs with stones or burnt bricks, or to write a verse of the Qurán upon them, is forbidden in the Hadís; but large stone and brick tombs are common to all Muhammadan countries, and very frequently they bear inscriptions.

On the third day after the burial of the dead, it is usual for the relatives to visit the grave, and to recite selections from the Qurán. Those who can afford to pay Maulavís, employ these learned men to recite the whole of the Qurán at the graves of their deceased relatives; and,

---

* *Vide* article on Angels.

as we have already remarked, in a former article, the Qurán is divided into sections to admit of its being recited by the several Maulavís at once. During the days of mourning the relatives abstain from wearing any article of dress of a bright colour, and their soiled garments remain unchanged.

XLII.—SLAVERY.

SLAVERY (*'ubudíyat*) has been consecrated by Muhammadan law, and some of its provisions have been taken from the Mosaic code. The traces of heathenism are, however, observable in most of the Muslim laws with reference to this question. For example, according to Jewish law,* if a master slew his slave he was liable to punishment, whereas the Islamic code † annexes no worldly punishment for the murder of a slave.

There is no limit to the number of slave girls with whom a Muslim may cohabit, and it is the *consecration* of this illimitable indulgence which so popularizes slavery amongst Muhammadan nations. Some Muslim writers ‡ of the

---

* Exodus xxi. 20.
† Hidáya, bk. xvi.
‡ Life of Muhammad, by Sayyid Ameer Ali, p. 257. It

present day contend that Muhammad looked upon the custom as temporary in its nature, and held that its extinction was sure to be achieved by the progress of ideas and change of circumstances; but the slavery of Islám is interwoven with the Law of marriage, the Law of sale, and the Law of inheritance, of the system, and its abolition would strike at the very foundations of the code of Muhammadanism.

Slavery is in complete harmony with the spirit of Islám, whilst it is abhorrent to that of Christianity. That Muhammad ameliorated the condition of the slave, as it existed under the heathen laws of Arabia, we cannot doubt; but it is equally certain that the Arabian legislator intended it to be a perpetual institution.

The following traditions * with reference to the action of the Prophet in this matter are notable :—

" 'Imrán-ibn-Husain said a man freed six

---

is often said that the buying and selling of slaves is not sanctioned by Islám; this is not correct, as will be seen upon reference to the Muhammadan Law of Sale.

* Mishkát, bk. xiii. chap. xx. pt. 1.

slaves at his death, and he had no other property besides; and the Prophet called them, and divided them into three sections, and then cast lots; he then ordered that two of them should be freed, and he retained four in slavery, and spoke severely of the man who had set them free."

"Jábir said we used to sell the mothers of children in the time of the Prophet, and of Abu Bakr; but Omar forbade it in his time."

For certain sins the manumission of slaves is the legal penalty, and a slave may purchase his own freedom with *the permission of his owner.*

In the Akhlák-i-Jilálí,* which is the popular work upon practical philosophy amongst the Muhammadans, it is said that "for service a slave is preferable to a freeman, inasmuch as he must be more disposed to submit, obey, and adopt his patron's habits and pursuits."

Although slavery has existed side by side with Christianity, it is undoubtedly contrary to the spirit of the teaching of our divine Lord,

---

* Akhlák-i-Jalálí, by Fakír Jáni Muhammad Asa'ad, sect. 6.

who has given to the world the grand doctrine of universal brotherhood.

Mr. Lecky believes * that it was the spirit of Christianity which brought about the abolition of slavery in Europe. He says, "The services of Christianity were of three kinds. It supplied a new order of relations, in which the distinction of classes was unknown. It imparted a moral dignity to the servile classes. It gave an unexampled impetus to the movement of enfranchisement."

---

* History of European Morals, vol. ii. p. 70.

XLIII.—THE KHUTBAH, OR THE FRIDAY'S SERMON.

THE *Khutbah* is the oration or sermon delivered in the mosque every Friday, and on the chief festivals,* after the meridian prayer. After the usual ablutions, the four *Sunnat* prayers are recited. The *Khatíb*, or preacher, then seats himself on the *Mimbar* (pulpit), whilst the Muazzin proclaims the Azán; after which he stands up on the second step,† and delivers

---

* The 'Id-i-Fitr and the 'Id-ul-Azhá.

† The Mimbar is the pulpit of a mosque. It consists of three steps, and is sometimes a moveable wooden structure, and sometimes a fixture of brick or stone built against the wall. Muhammad, in addressing the congregation, stood on the uppermost step, Abu Bakr on the second, and Omar on the third or the lowest. Osmán, being the most modest of the Khalifs, would have gladly descended lower if he could have done so; but this being impossible, he fixed upon the second step, from which it is still the custom to preach.

the sermon, which must be in the Arabic language, and include prayers for "Muhammad, the Companions, and the King." There are several books of *Khutbahs* published for the use of preachers. The most celebrated of these preachers' manuals is the Mujmua' Khitáb, printed by Abdur Rahman of Cawnpore. The sermons are arranged for every Friday in the year, and are the compositions of various Muslim divines. It is remarkable that short sermons are meritorious; for it is related that the "Prophet" remarked that "the length of a man's prayers and the shortness of his sermon are the signs of his sense and understanding; therefore make your prayers long and your Khutbah short."

The following is a translation of the third Khutbah in the book of sermons already mentioned; it is a fair specimen of an average Khutbah, both as to its length and matter :—

"In the name of God, the compassionate, the merciful.

"Praised be God. Praised be that God who hath shown us the way in this religion. If He had not guided us into the path we should not have found it.

"I bear witness that there is no deity but God. He is one. He has no associate. I bear witness that Muhammad is, of a truth, His servant and His Apostle. May God have mercy upon him, and upon his descendants, and upon his companions, and give them peace.

"Fear God, O ye people, and fear *that* day, the day of judgment, when a father will not be able to answer for his son, nor the son for the father. Of a truth God's promises are true. Let not this present life make you proud. Let not the deceiver (Satan) lead you astray.

"O ye people who have believed, turn ye to God, as Nasuá* did turn to God. Verily God doth forgive all sin, verily He is the merciful, the forgiver of sins. Verily He is the most munificent, and bountiful, the King, the Holy One, the Clement, the Most Merciful."

The preacher then descends from the pulpit, and sitting on the floor of the mosque, offers

---

* *Nasuá*, is a name which occurs in the sixth verse of the Súrat-i-Tahrímah (lxvi.) in the Qurán; it is translated "true repentance" by Sale and Rodwell, but it is supposed to be a person's name by several commentators.

up a silent prayer. He then, again, ascends the *Mimbar*, as before, and proceeds thus:—

"In the name of God, the compassionate, the merciful.

"Praised be God. We praise Him. We seek help from Him. We ask forgiveness of sins. We trust in Him. We seek refuge in Him from evil desires and from former sinful actions. He who has God for his guide is never lost; and whomsoever He leadeth aside none can guide into the right path.

"We bear witness that there is no deity but God. He is one. He hath no partner.

"Verily we bear witness that Muhammad is the servant and apostle of God, and may God have mercy upon him, who is more exalted than any being. May God have mercy upon his descendants, and upon his companions May God give them peace! Especially upon Amír-ul-Mominín Abu Bakr Sadíq (may God be pleased with him). And upon him who was the most temperate of the "friends" Amír-ul-Mominín Omar Ibn-ul-Khattáb (may God be pleased with him). And upon him whose modesty and faith were perfect, Amír-ul-Mominín Osmán (may God be pleased with him). And upon the Lion of the powerful God, Amír-ul-Mominín Ali ibn Abu-Tálib (may God be pleased with him). And upon the two Imáms, the holy ones, the two martyrs, Amír-ul-Mominín Abu Muhammad Hasan and Abu Abdullah Husain (may God be pleased with both of them). And upon the mother of these two persons, the chief of women, Fatimah-uz-Zárah (may God be pleased with her). And upon his (Muhammad's) two uncles, Hamza and 'Abbás (may God be pleased with them). And upon the rest of the "companions," and upon the "followers" (may God be pleased with all of them). Of Thy mercy, O most merciful of all merciful ones, O God, forgive all Musalmán men and Musalmán women, all male believers, and all female believers. Of a truth thou art He who wilt receive our prayers.

"O God, help those who help the religion of Muhammad. May we also exert ourselves to help those who help Islám. Make those weak, who weaken the religion of Muhammad.

"O God, bless the king of the age, and make him kind and favourable to the people.

"O servants of God, may God have mercy

upon you. Verily, God enjoineth justice and the doing of good, and gifts to kindred; and He forbiddeth wickedness, and wrong, and oppression. He warneth you that haply ye may be mindful.*

"O ye people, remember the great and exalted God. He will also remember you. He will answer your prayers. The remembrance of God is great, and good, and honourable, and noble, and meritorious, and worthy, and sublime."

The preacher then descends, and taking up his position as Imám, facing the *Mihráb*,† conducts two *rak'at* prayers. The Khatíb, however, does not always officiate as Imám.

In the above Khutbah we have inserted the petition usually offered up in behalf of "the king" in India, although it does not occur in the collection of sermons from which we have translated. Until the Mutiny of 1857,

---

* The ninety-second verse of Súrat-i-Nahe (cxvi.) of the Qurán.

† The Mihráb is the centre of the wall of a mosque, facing Mecca, to which the Imám (priest) prays. It usually consists of a circular niche in the wall.

we believe that in the majority of mosques in North India it was recited in the name of the King of Delhi, and even now we are informed that some bigoted Imáms say it in the name of the Sultan of Turkey. The recital of the Khutbah serves to remind every Muhammadan priest, at least once a week, that he is in the land of warfare (*Dár-ul-Harb*); and the fact that Muhammadans under Christian rule are in an anomalous position, is a source of trouble to many a conscientious Muslim. A few years ago, a celebrated Muhammadan divine sent for a native Christian officer, as he wished to obtain his aid in an important matter. The nature of the good man's difficulty was as follows:—The Friday prayer, or Khutbah, must, according to Muhammadan law, be said in the name and by the *permission* of the ruler of the land. He had been saying the Friday prayer without permission of the ruler, and he feared that these prayers had, consequently, not been accepted by the Almighty. He, therefore, asked the Christian officer to obtain the necessary permission from the magistrate of the district. The Christian was also a man versed in Muslim law, and he quoted authorities to prove that

THE KHUTBAH, OR THE FRIDAY'S SERMON. 205

the permission of an "infidel" ruler was not what Islám enjoined.

In Turkey and Egypt, and in other countries under Muslim rule, it is the custom for the Khatíb to deliver the Khutbah whilst he holds a wooden sword reversed.

The prayer for the reigning monarch, if he be a Muslim, would be offered up in the following manner:—

"O God, aid Islám, and strengthen its pillars, and make infidelity to tremble, and destroy its might, by the preservation of Thy servant, and the son of Thy servant, the submissive to the might of Thy Majesty and Glory, whom God hath aided, our master Amír Sher 'Alí Khán, son of Amír Dost Muhammad Khán, may God assist him and prolong his reign. O God, assist him, and assist his armies. O Thou God of the religion and Lord of the world, assist the armies of Muslims; frustrate the armies of infidels and polytheists, thine enemies, the enemies of the religion."

XLIV.—JIHA'D, OR RELIGIOUS WAR.

JIHA'D* (lit. "an effort") is a religious war against the infidels, as enjoined by Muhammad in the following passages in the Qurán:—

Súrat-un-Nisá (vi.).

> "Fight, therefore, for the religion of God."
>
> * * * * *
>
> God hath indeed promised Paradise to every one,
> But God hath preferred those who *fight for the faith.*"

Súrat-ul-Muhammad (xlvii.).

> "Those who *fight in defence of God's true religion,*
> God will not suffer their works to perish."

Those who engage in war against the infidels are called *Ghazís*. The whole question of *Jihád* has been fully discussed by Dr. W. W. Hunter, of the Bengal Civil Service, in his work entitled, "Indian Musalmáns," which is the re-

---

* Some Muhammadan divines say there are two Jiháds, *viz.* Jihád-ul-Akbar, or the Greater Warfare, which is against one's own lusts; and Jihád-ul-Asghar, or the Lesser Warfare, against infidels.

sult of careful inquiry as to the necessary conditions of a Jihád, or Cresentade, instituted at the time of the excitement which existed in India in 1870-71, in consequence of a supposed Wahhábí conspiracy for the overthrow of Christian rule in that country. The whole matter, according to the Sunní Musulmáns, hinges upon the question whether India is *Dár-ul-Harb*, the land of enmity, or *Dár-ul-Islám*, the land of Islám.

The Muftís belonging to the Hanifia and Shafa'ía sects at Mecca decided that, "as long as even some of the peculiar observances of Islám prevail in a country, it is *Dár-ul-Islám*."

The decision of the Muftí of the Málikí sect was very similar, being to the following effect:—

" A country does not become *Dár-ul-Harb* as soon as it passes into the hands of the infidels, but when all or most of the injunctions of Islám disappear therefrom."

The law doctors of North India decided that, "the absence of protection and liberty to Musulmáns is essential in a *Jihád*, or religious war, and that there should be a probability of victory to the armies of Islám."

The Shía'h decision on the subject was as

follows:—"A Jihád is lawful only when the armies of Islám are led by the rightful Imám, when arms and ammunitions of war and experienced warriors are ready, when it is against the enemies of God, when he who makes war is in possession of his reason, and when he has secured the permission of his parents, and has sufficient money to meet the expenses of his journey."

The Sunnís and Shía'hs alike believe in the eventual triumph of Islám, when the whole world shall become followers of the Prophet of Arabia; but whilst the Sunnís are, of course, ready to undertake the accomplishment of this great end, " whenever there is a probability of victory to the Musulmáns," the Shía'hs, true to the one great principle of their sect, must wait until the appearance of a rightful Imám.

Not very long ago a learned Muhammadan *Qází* (judge) was consulted by the writer of these notes with reference to this interesting question, namely, whether India is *Dár-ul-Islám*, or *Dár-ul-Harb*. At first he replied *Dár-ul-Islám*, and then, after a short pause, he said, " Well, sir, may I tell you the truth?" Upon being assured that the question was put merely as one of theological inquiry, and not for any political reasons, he replied, "It is *Dár-ul-Harb*." One of his reasons for arriving at this conclusion was the well-known doctrine of Islám that a Muslim cannot be a *Zimmí*, or one who pays tribute to an infidel power. We believe that the fact that Muhammadans under Christian rule are in an anomalous position, is a source of trouble to many a conscientious Muslim. Many Muslims believe that *Hijrat*, or flight, is incumbent upon every child of *the Faith* who is under Káfir (infidel) rule; but, as our friend the Qází put it, "Where are they to go to?" The Muslim who abandons his country under such circumstances is called a *Muhájir*, or refugee.

When an infidel's country is conquered by a Muslim ruler, its inhabitants are offered three alternatives :—

(1.) *The reception of Islám*, in which case the conquered become enfranchised citizens of the Muslim state.

(2.) *The payment of a poll-tax* (*Jizíyah*), by which unbelievers in Islám obtain protection, and become *Zimmís*.

(3.) *Death by the sword.*

In a state brought under Muslims, all those who do not embrace the faith are placed under certain disabilities. They can worship God according to their own customs, *provided they are not idolaters;* but it must be done without any ostentation, and, whilst churches and synagogues may be repaired, *no new place of worship can be erected.* *Vide* Hidáyah,* where we read:—"The construction of churches, or synagogues, in Muslim territory is unlawful, this being forbidden in the Traditions; but if places of worship belonging to Jews, or Christians, be destroyed, or fall into decay, they are at liberty to repair them, because buildings cannot endure for ever."

Idol temples must be destroyed, and idolatry suppressed by force in all countries ruled according to strict Muslim law.

---

* Hamilton's Translation, vol. ii. p. 219.

XLV.—MARTYRS.

THE title of *Shahíd*, or martyr, is given to anyone who dies under the following circumstances :—

1. A soldier who dies in war for the cause of Islám.
2. One who innocently meets with his death from the hand of another.
3. The victim of a plague.
4. A person accidentally drowned.
5. One upon whom a wall may fall accidentally.
6. A person burnt in a house on fire.
7. One who dies from hunger.
8. One who dies on the pilgrimage to Mecca.

If a martyr dies in war, or is innocently murdered, he is buried without the usual washing before burial, as it is said that the blood of a martyr is a sufficient ablution.

XLVI.—THE FOUR ORTHODOX SECTS.

There are four orthodox sects or schools of interpretation amongst the Sunnís, the Hanifí, the Sháfa'í, the Málikí, and the Hambalí.

1. The Hanifís are found in Turkey, Central Asia, and North India. The founder of this sect was Imám Abu Hanífa, who was born at Koofa, the capital of Irák, A.D. 702, or A.H. 80, at which time four of the "Prophet's" companions were still alive. He is the great oracle of jurisprudence, and (with his two pupils Imám Abu Yusaf and Imám Muhammad) was the founder of the Hanifí Code of Law.*

2. The Sháfa'ías are found in South India and Egypt. The founder of this school of interpretation was Imám Muhammad ibn i Idrís al

---

* A Digest of the Hanifí Code of Law has been published in English by Mr. N. B. E. Baillie.

Shafa'í, who was born at Askalon, in Palestine, A.D. 772 (A.H. 150).

3. The Málikís prevail in Morocco, Barbary, and other parts of Africa, and were founded by Imám Málik, who was born at Madina, A.D. 716 (A.H. 93). He enjoyed the personal acquaintance of Hanífa, and he was considered the most learned man of his time.

4. The Hambalis were founded by Imám Abu 'Abdulláh Ahmad ibn Muhammad ibn Hambal, who was born at Bagdad, A.D. 786 (A.H. 164). He attended the lectures delivered by Shafa'í, by whom he was instructed in the traditions. His followers are found in Eastern Arabia, and in some parts of Africa, but it is the least popular of the four schools of interpretation. They have no Muftí at Mecca, whilst the other three sects are represented there. The Wahhábís rose from this sect.

From the disciples of these four great Imáms have proceeded an immense number of commentaries and other works, all differing on a variety of points in their constructions, although coinciding in their general principles.

XLVII.—THE SHI'A'HS.

THE Shía'hs (lit. "followers") are the followers of 'Ali, the husband of Fatimah, the daughter of Muhammad. They maintain that 'Ali was the first legitimate Khalífa, or successor to Muhammad, and therefore reject Abu Bakr, Omar, and Osmán, the first three Khalifs, as usurpers. According to the Shía'hs the Muslim religion consists of a knowledge of the true *Imám*, or leader, and the differences amongst themselves with reference to this question have given rise to endless divisions. Of the proverbial seventy-three sects of Islám, not fewer than thirty-two are assigned to the Shía'hs.

The twelve Imáms, according to the Shía'hs, are as follows:—

1. Hazrat 'Ali.
2. Hasan.
3. Husain.
4. Zain-ul-'Abid-dín.
5. Muhammad Báqr.

6. Jáfir Sádiq.
7. Músa Kázim.
8. 'Ali Músa Razá.
9. Muhammad Taqí.
10. Muhammad Naqí.
11. Hasan 'Askarí.
12. Abu Qásim (or Imám Mahdí).

The last Imám, Abu Qásim, is supposed by the Shía'hs to be still alive and concealed in some secret place; and that he is the same Mahdí, or director, concerning whom Muhammad prophesied that the world should not have an end until one of his own descendants should govern the Arabians, and whose coming in the last days is expected by all Muslims.

During the absence of the Imám, the Shía'hs appeal to the *Mujtahids*, or enlightened doctors of the law, for direction in all matters both temporal and spiritual. Since the accession of Ismaíl, the first of the Sufí dynasty, A.D. 1499, the Shía'h faith has been the national religion of Persia. The enmity which exists between Sunní and Shía'h Muhammadans is, perhaps, hardly equalled by the mutual animosity which too often exists between Romanists and Protestants.

It is not true that the Shía'h Muhammadans reject the Traditions of Muhammad, although the Sunnís arrogate to themselves the title of traditionists. They do not acknowledge the *Siháh-i-Sita*, or six correct books of the Sunnís and Wahhábís, but receive the five collections of Traditions, entitled: 1. Káfi; 2. Man-lá-yastahzirah-al-Faqíh; 3. Tahzíb; 4. Istibsár; 5. Nahaj-ul-Balághat.

The Shía'h school of law is called the Imámía,* and it is earlier than that of the Sunnís; for Abu Hanífa, the father of the Sunní code of law, received his first instructions in jurisprudence from Imám Jáfir Sádiq, the sixth Imám of the Shía'hs; but this learned doctor afterwards separated from his teacher, and established a school of his own.

The differences between the Shía'hs and Sunnís are very numerous, but we will enumerate a few of them:—

1. The discussion as to the office of Imám, already alluded to.

2. The Shía'hs have a profound veneration

---

* A Digest of the Imámía code has been published by Mr. N. B. E. Baillie. London, 1869.

for Imám 'Ali, and some of their sects regard him as an incarnation of divinity. They all assert that next to the Prophet, 'Ali is the most excellent of men.

3. They observe the ceremonies of the Muharram in commemoration of 'Ali, Hasan, Husain, and Bíbí Fatimah, whilst the Sunnís only regard the tenth day of Muharram, the *'A'shúráa*, being the day on which God is said to have created Adam and Eve, etc.

4. The Shía'hs permit Muta'h, or temporary marriages, which are contracted for a limited period, and for a certain sum of money. The Sunnís say that Muhammad afterwards cancelled this institution.

5. The Shía'hs include the *Majusí*, or fire-worshippers, among the *Ahl-i-Kitáb*, or people of the Book, whilst Sunnís only acknowledge Jews, Christians, and Muslims, as *Kitábíahs*.

6. There are also various minor differences in the ceremony of *Sulát*, or prayer, and in the ablutions previous to prayer.

7. The Shía'hs admit a principle of religious compromise which is called *Takía* (lit. "guarding one's self"), a pious fraud, whereby the Shía'h Muhammadan believes he is justified

in either smoothing down or in denying the peculiarities of his religious belief in order to save himself from religious persecution. A Shía'h can, therefore, pass himself off as a Sunní, or even curse the twelve Imáms, in order to avoid persecution.

XLVIII.—THE WAHHA'BI'S.

THIS sect was founded by Muhammad, son of Abdul Wahháb, but as their opponents could not call them *Muhammadans*, they have been distinguished by the name of the father of the founder of their sect, and are called Wahhábís.*

Shekh Muhammad was born at Ayína, a village in the province, of Arad, in the country of Najd, in the year A.D. 1691. Having been carefully instructed in the tenets of the Muslim religion, according to the teachings of the Hambalí sect, he in due time left his native place, in company with his father, to perform the pilgrimage to Mecca. At Madina, he was instructed by Shekh Abdullah-ibn-Ibrahím, of Najd; and, it is supposed, that whilst sitting at the feet of this celebrated teacher, the

---

* *Vide* a Wahhábí book entitled Sulh-ul-Aklwán, by Sayyid Allama Daud, of Bagdad.

son of Abdul Wahháb first realized how far the rigid lines of Islám had been stretched, almost to breaking, in the endeavour to adapt its stern principles to the superstitions of idolatrous Arabia. He accompanied his father to Harimala, and, after his father's death, he returned to his native village of Ayína, where he assumed the position of a religious teacher. His teachings met with acceptance, and he soon acquired so great an influence over the people of those parts that the Governor of Hassa compelled him to leave the district, and the reformer found a friendly asylum in Deraiah, under the protection of Muhammad-ibn-Saud, a chief of considerable influence, who made the protection of Ibn-Abdul-Wahháb a pretext for a war with the Shekh of Hassa. Ibn Saud married the daughter of Ibn-Abdul-Wahháb, and established in his family the Wahhábí dynasty, which, after a chequered existence of more than a hundred years, still exists in the person of the Wahhábí chief at Ryadh.*

---

* The following are the names of the Wahhábí chiefs, from the establishment of the dynasty:—Muhammad-ibn-Saud, died A.D. 1765; Abdul-Azíz, assassinated 1803;

The whole of Eastern Arabia has embraced the reformed doctrines of the Wahhábís, and Mr. Palgrave, in his account of his travels in those parts, has given an interesting sketch of the Wahhábí religionists, although he is not always correct as to the distinctive principles of their religious creed.

In the great Wahhábí revival, political interests were united with religious reform, as was the case in the great Puritan struggle in England; and the Wahhábís soon pushed their conquests over the whole of Arabia. In A.D. 1803, they conquered Mecca and Madina, and for many years threatened the subjugation of the whole Turkish empire; but in A.D. 1811, Muhammad 'Ali, the celebrated Pasha of Egypt, commenced a war against the Wahhábís, and soon recovered Mecca and Madina; and in 1818, his son, Ibrahím Pasha, totally defeated Abdullah, the Wahhábí leader, and

---

Saud-ibn-Abdul Azíz, died 1814; Abdullah-ibn-Saud, beheaded 1818; Turkí, assassinated 1830; Fayzul, died 1866; Abdullah, still living. Fayzul and his son Abdullah entertained Col. Sir Lewis Pelly, K.C.B., K.C.S.I., who visited the Wahhábí capital, as Her Britannic Majesty's representative, in 1865.

sent him a prisoner to Constantinople, where he was executed in the public square of St. Sophia, December 19th, 1818. But although the temporal power of the Wahhábís has been subdued, they still continue secretly to propagate their peculiar tenets, and in the present day there are numerous disciples of the sect not only in Arabia, but in Turkey and in India. It is a movement which has influenced religious thought in every part of Islám.

The leader of the Wahhábí movement in India was Sayyid Ahmad, who was born at Ráí Barelí, in Oudh, in A.D. 1786. He began life as a freebooter; but about the year 1816, he gave up robbery, and commenced to study divinity in one of the mosques at Delhi. After a few years study, he performed the pilgrimage to the sacred city; and, whilst at Mecca, attracted the notice of the learned doctors by the similarity of his teaching to that of the Wahhábí sectaries, from whom the city had suffered so much. He was soon expelled from the town, and he returned to India a fanatical disciple of the Wahhábí leader. His success as a preacher was great, both in Bombay and Calcutta; and having collected a numerous following from the ranks of Islám within British territory, he proceeded to the north-west frontier of India, and preached a Jihád, or Holy War, against the Sikhs. On the 21st of December 1826, the war against the infidel Sikhs began, and almost every place in the Peshawur valley is, in some way, associated with this fanatical struggle. The mission of this Wahhábí leader was soon brought to an untimely end; for, in the battle of Bálakot, in Hazarah, in May 1831, when the fanatics were surprised by a Sikh army, under Sher Singh, their leader, Sayyid Ahmad, was slain.* But, as in the case of the Wahhábí leader of Eastern Arabia, the propagation of the religious tenets did not cease with Sayyid Ahmad's death, and within the last thirty years Wahhábyism has widely influenced religious thought amongst the Muhammadans of India. The people who hold the doctrines of the Wahhábís do not always combine with them the fanatical spirit of either the son of Abdul Wahháb, or

---

* The remnant of the Sayyid's army formed the nucleus of the Wahhábí fanatics, who are now stationed at the village of Polosí, on the banks of the Indus, on the north-west frontier of British India.

of Sayyid Ahmad Khán; they speak of themselves as *Ahl-i-Hadís*, or the people of the traditions, or those who interpret the teaching of the Qurán by the example of Muhammad; but there can be but little doubt that the religious principles of the Wahhábís of India are identical with those of the Wahhábís of Arabia, although it does not follow that they are imbued with exactly the same fanatical spirit. It must, however, be remembered that there is no separation between Church and State in the principles of Islám, and that Muhammadans only cease to be fanatical and disloyal under foreign rule when they are certain that opportunities for resistance do not exist. In the *fatwá* (decision) given by a number of learned doctors of Lucknow and other places, dated 17th July 1870, it was stated that " *it is necessary that there should be a probability of victory to the Musalmáns, and glory to the people of Hindustán. If there be no such probability, the Jihád is unlawful.*" *

---

* *Vide* Hunter's Indian Musalmáns, Appendix II. Dr. Badger, in his article in the "Contemporary Review," June 1875, questions whether there is any real affinity between the Wahhabyism of India and Najd, but we believe they are identical in principle and spirit.

The Wahhábís speak of themselves as *Muwahhid*, or Unitarians, and call all others *Mushrik*, or those who associate another with God; and the following are some of their distinctive religious tenets :—

1. They do not receive the decisions of the four orthodox sects, but say that any man who can read and understand the Qurán and the sacred Hadís can judge for himself in matters of doctrine. They, therefore, reject *Ijma'* after the death of the Companions of the Prophet.

2. That no one but God can know the secrets of men, and that prayers should not be offered to any Prophet, Walí, Pír, or Saint; but that God may be asked to grant a petition for the *sake* of a saint.

3. That at the last day, Muhammad will obtain permission (*izn*) of God to intercede for his people. The Sunnís believe that permission has already been given.

4. That it is unlawful to illuminate the shrines of departed saints, or to prostrate before them, or to perambulate (*tawáf*) round them.

5. That women should not be allowed to visit the graves of the dead, on account of their immoderate weeping.

6. That only four festivals ought to be observed, namely, 'Id-ul-Fitr, 'Id-ul-Azhá, 'A'shúráa, and Shab-i-Barát.

7. They do not observe the ceremonies of *Maulúd*, which are celebrated on the anniversary of Muhammad's birth.

8. They do not present offerings (*Nazr*) at any shrine.

9. They count the ninety-nine names of God on their fingers, and not on a rosary.

10. They understand the terms "sitting of God," and "hand of God," which occur in the Qurán, in their literal (*Haqíqí*) sense, and not figuratively (*Majází*); but, at the same time, they say it is not revealed *how* God sits, or in what sense he has a hand, etc.*

---

* On this account the Christian doctrines of the Trinity and the Sonship of Christ do not present the same difficulties to the mind of a Wahhábí which they do to that of a Sunní.

XLIX.—SUFI'ISM, OR MYSTICISM.

THE term *Súfí* is said to be derived from the Arabic *Súf*, "wool," on account of the woollen garments worn by the Eastern ascetics; or from the Persian *Sáf*, "pure," with reference to the Sufiistic effort to attain to metaphysical purity; or from the Greek, σοφια, "wisdom," *i. e.* the true wisdom, or knowledge.

Tasawwaf, or Sufíism, appears to be but the Muslim adaptation of the doctrines of the Vedanta school, which we also find in the writings of the old academies of Greece, and which Sir William Jones thought Plato learned from the sages of the East.

The Súfís are divided into innumerable sects; but although they differ in name, and in some of their customs, they are all agreed in the principal tenets, especially those which inculcate the absolute necessity of blind submission to an inspired teacher, or *Murshid*. They believe that God only exists. He is in all things, and all things in Him, and all created beings visible and invisible are an emanation from God, and not really distinct from Him. That the soul of man existed before the body in which it is confined as in a cage. The great object of the Súfí being to escape from the trammels of humanity, and to return to the bosom of divinity, whilst the teachings of their mystic creed are supposed to lead the soul onward, stage by stage, until it reaches the goal—*perfect knowledge.*

The natural state of every Muslim is *Násút,* in which state the disciple must observe the precepts of the law, or *Shari'at*; but, as this is the lowest form of spiritual existence, the performance of the *journey* is enjoined upon every searcher after Truth.

The following are the stages (*Manzil*) which the Súfí has to perform. Having become a searcher after God (*Tálib*), he enters the first stage of '*Ubúdíyat,* " service." When the Divine attraction has developed his inclination into the love of God, he is said to have reached the second stage of '*Ishaq,* "love." This Divine love, expelling all worldly desires from his heart, he arrives at the third stage of *Zuhd*, "seclusion." Occupying himself henceforward with contemplation and the investigations of the metaphysical theories concerning the nature, attributes, and works of God, which are the characteristics of the Súfí system, he reaches the fourth stage of *M'arifat*, "knowledge." This assiduous contemplation of metaphysical theories soon produces a state of mental excitement, which is considered a sure prognostication of direct illumination from God. This fifth stage is called *Wajd*, "ecstasy." During the next stage he is supposed to receive a revelation of the true nature of the Godhead, and to have reached the sixth stage of *Haqíqat*, "truth." The next stage is that of *Wasl*, "union with God," which is the highest stage to which he can go whilst in the body; but when death overtakes him, it is looked upon as a total re-absorption into the Deity, forming the consummation of his journey and the eighth and last stage of *Faná*, "extinction." That stage in which the traveller is said to have attained to the love of God, is the point from which the Sufiistic poets love to discuss the doctrines of their sect. The *Sálik*, or traveller, is the Lover (*'A'shiq*), and God is the Beloved One (*M'ashuq*). This Divine love is the theme of most of the Persian and Pushtu poems, which abound in Sufiistic expressions which are difficult of interpretation to an ordinary English reader. For instance, *Sharáb*, "wine," expresses the domination of Divine love in the heart. *Gísú*, "a ringlet," the details of the mysteries of Divinity. *Mai Khána*, "a tavern," a stage of the journey. "Mirth," "wantonness," and "inebriation," signify religious enthusiasm and abstraction from worldly things.

The eight stages which we have given are those usually taught by Súfí teachers in their published works; but in North India we have frequently met with persons of this sect, who have learnt only the four following stages:—

The first, *Násút*, "humanity," for which there is the *Shari'at*, or law. The second *Malakút*, "the nature of angels," for which there is *Taríqat*, or the pathway of purity. The third is *Jabarút*, "the possession of power," for which there is *M'arifat*, or knowledge. And the fourth is *Láhút*, "extinction," for which there is *Haqíqat*, or truth.

The Súfí mystic seeks, by concentration of

his thoughts and affections on God, to lose his own identity; and the following fable, related by Jalál-ud-dín, the author of the Masnawí,* illustrates their views on the subject. It represents Human Love seeking admission into the Sanctuary of Divinity :—

"One knocked at the door of the Beloved, and a voice from within inquired 'Who is there?' Then he answered, '*It is I.*' And the voice said, 'This house will not hold me and thee.' So the door remained shut. Then the Lover sped away into the wilderness, and fasted and prayed in solitude. And after a year he returned, and knocked again at the door, and the voice again demanded, 'Who is there?' And the Lover said, '*It is Thou.*' Then the door was opened."

In Professor Max Müller's address to the Aryan section of the International Congress of Orientalists assembled in London, in September, 1874, he said:—"We have learnt already one lesson, that behind the helpless expressions

---

* The Masnawí is the celebrated book of the Súfí mystics which, it is said, takes the place of the Qurán amongst the majority of people in Persia.

which language has devised, whether in the East or the West, for uttering the unutterable * * * there is the same intention, the same striving, the same stammering, the same faith. Other lessons will follow, till in the end we shall be able to restore that ancient word which unites not only the East with the West, but with all the members of the human family, and may learn to understand what a Persian poet meant when he wrote many centuries ago :—' Diversity of worship has divided the human race into seventy-two nations. From all their dogmas I have selected one—the love of God.' "

By "the seventy-two * (seventy-three?) nations," are doubtless meant the number of sects into which Muhammad said Islám would be divided; but the learned Professor surely cannot be ignorant of the fact that the "*love of God*," selected by the Persian poet, as the dogma *par excellence*, is the '*Ishaq*, or second

---

* Muhammad said that, as the Jews had been divided into seventy-one sects, and the Christians into seventy-two, the Muslims would be divided into seventy-three, that is seventy-two in addition to the "*orthodox*," or *Nájiah* sect, each sect, of course, claiming to be *Nájiah*.

stage of the Sufiistic journey. Only those who have conversed with Súfís on this mystical love can well realize how impossible it is for the Christian to reconcile that practical love *of* God, which "gave His only begotten Son," and that practical love *to* God, which is shown by keeping His commandments, with that mystical love, or *'Ishaq*, which is the subject of Súfí divinity.

L.—FAQI'RS, OR DARWESHES.

The Arabic word *Faqír*, signifies poor; but it is used in the sense of being in need of mercy, and poor in the sight of God, rather than in need of worldly assistance. *Darwesh* is derived from the Persian *dar*, "a door,"—those who beg from door to door. The terms are generally used for those who lead a religious life. Religious Faqírs are divided into two great classes, the *ba Shara'* (with the law), or those who govern their conduct according to the principles of Islám; and the *be Shara'* (without the law), or those who do not rule their lives according to the principles of any religious creed, although they call themselves Musulmáns. The former are called *Sálik*, or travellers on the pathway (*taríqat*) to heaven; and the latter are either *A'zád* (free), or *Majzúb* (abstracted). The *Sálik* embrace the various religious orders who perform the Zikrs described in our next note. The *Majzúb* are totally absorbed in religious reverie. The *A'zád* shave their beards, whiskers, moustachios, eyebrows and eyelashes, and lead lives of celibacy.

The *A'zád* and *Majzúb* Faqírs can scarcely be said to be Muhammadans, so that a description of their various sects do not fall within the limits of these notes. The Sálik Faqírs are also divided into very numerous orders; but their chief difference consists in their *Silsilah*, or chain of succession, from their great teachers the Khalífas 'Ali, and Abu Bakr, who are said to have been the founders of the religious order of Faqírs. European writers have distinguished the various orders by their dress and their religious performances; but we have not been able to find that these are the distinguishing features of difference amongst them.

The following are the chief orders which are met with in North India :—

1. The Naqshbandía are followers of Khwájah Pír Muhammad Naqshband, and are a very numerous sect; they usually perform the *Zikr-i-Khafí*, or the silent religious devotion described in the next chapter.

2. The Qádiría sprung from the celebrated Sayyid Abdul Qádir, surnamed Pír Dustagír, whose shrine is at Bagdad. They practise both the *Zikr-i-Jalí*, and the *Zikr-i-Khafí*. Most of the Sunní Maulavís on the north-west frontier of India are members of this order. In Egypt it is most popular amongst fishermen.

3. The Chishtía are followers of Banda Nawáz, surnamed the *Gaysu daráz*, or the long-ringletted. His shrine is at Calburgah.

The Shía'hs generally become Faqírs of this order. They are partial to vocal music, for the founder of the order remarked, that singing was the food and support of the soul. They perform the *Zikr-i-Jalí*, described in the next article.

4. The Jalália were founded by Sayyid Jalál-ud-dín, of Bokhára. They are met with in Central Asia. Religious mendicants are often of this order.

5. The Sarwardía are a popular order in Afghanistan, and comprise a number of learned men. They are the followers of Hasan Bisrí, of Basra, near Bagdad.

These are the most noted orders of *ba Shara'* Faqírs. The *be Shara'* Faqírs are very nume-

FAQIRS, OR DARWESHES. 237

rous. The most popular order is that of the *Mudária*, founded by Zinda Sháh Murdár, of Syria, whose shrine is at Mukanpur, in Oudh. From these have sprung the *Malang* Faqírs who crowd the bazaars of India. They wear their hair matted and tied in a knot. The Rafía order is also a numerous one in some parts of India. They practise the most severe discipline, and mortify themselves by beating their bodies.

D'Ohsson enumerates thirty-two of the principal religious orders, giving the name of the founder, and the place of his shrine.

No.	Name of the Order.	Founder.	Place of the Founder's Shrine.	Date, A.H.
1	Alwání	Shekh Alwán	Jeddah	149
2	Adhamí	Ibrahím ibn Adham	Damascus	161
3	Bastámí	Bayazíd Bastámí	Jebel Bestámí	261
4	Saqatí	Sirrí Siqatí	Bagdad	295
5	Qádirí	Abdul-Qádir Jiláni	Bagdad	561
6	Rufálí	Syyid Ahmad Rufálí	Bagdad	576
7	Sahrwardí	Shiháb-ud-dín	Bagdad	602
8	Kabrawí	Najm-ud-dín	Khwaresm	617
9	Sházilí	Abul Hasan	Mecca	656
10	Maulaví	Jalál-ud-dín Muláná	Conyah	672
11	Badawí	Abul Fitan Ahmad	Egypt	675
12	Naqshbandí	Pír Muhammad	Persia	719
13	S'adí	S'ad-ud-dín	Damascus	736
14	Bakhtáshí	Hají Bakhtásh	Kír Sher	736
15	Khilwatí	'Umar Khilwatí	Caisarea	800
16	Zainí	Zain-ud-dín	Cufa	838
17	Baháí	Abdul Ghaní	Adrianople	870
18	Bairamí	Hají Bairam	Angora	876
19	Ashrafí	Ashraf Rumí	Chin Iznic	899
20	Bakrí	Abu Bakr Wafáí	Aleppo	902

No.	Name of the Order.	Founder.	Place of the Founder's Shrine.	Date, A.H.
21	Sunbulí	SunbulYusufBolawí	Constantinople	936
22	Ghulshaní	Ibrahím Ghulshaní	Cairo	940
23	Yíjit Báshí	Shams-ud-dín	Magnesia	951
24	Umm Sunání	Shekh Umm Sunán	Constantinople	959
25	Jalwatí	Pír Uftadí	Bursah	988
26	'Usháqí	Hasan-ud-dín	Constantinople	1001
27	Shamsí	Shams-ud-dín	Madina	1010
28	Sinan Ummí	'Alim Sinan Ummí	Elmahlí	1079
29	Níyází	Muhammad Niyáz	Lemnos	1100
30	Mas'adí	Murád Shámí	Constantinople	1132
31	Nuruddíní	Nur-ud-dín	Constantinople	1146
32	Jamálí	Jamál-ud-dín	Constantinople	1164

We insert the above list on the authority of M. D'Ohsson; but we have not had an opportunity of testing the correctness of its information.

The order of Maulavís is the most popular religious order in Constantinople. They are called by Europeans the dancing, or whirling darveshes, and their religious performances constitute one of the public sights in Constantinople. They have service at their *Takiya*, or convent, every Wednesday, and at Kasim Pasha every Sunday, at 2 o'clock. There are about twenty performers, with high round felt caps and brown mantles. At a given signal they all fall flat on their faces, and rise and walk slowly round and round with their arms folded, bowing and turning slowly several times. They then cast off their mantles and appear in long bell-shaped petticoats and jackets, and then begin to spin, revolving, dancing, and turning with extraordinary velocity.

The founder of this religious order was a native of Balkh, in Central Asia. It is said the spiritual powers of this extraordinary man were developed at the early age of six years; for once on a Friday Jalád-ud-dín was at Balkh on the roof of a house with some children of his own age, when one of the boys asked him if it were possible for him to jump from one house to the other. He replied, "If you have faith, jump up towards heaven." He then sprang upwards, and was immediately lost to sight. The youths all cried out as he disappeared, but he soon returned from the celestial regions, greatly altered in complexion and changed in figure; for he had obtained a sight of the abodes of bliss!

It is impossible to become acquainted with all the rules and ceremonies of the numerous orders of Faqírs; for, like those of the Freemasons, they may not be divulged to the uninitiated.

The following is said to be the usual method of admitting a Muhammadan to the order of a *ba Shara'* Faqír. Having first performed the legal ablutions, the *Muríd* (disciple) seats himself before the *Murshid* (spiritual guide). The Murshid then takes the Muríd's right hand, and requires of him a confession of sin according to the following form: "I ask forgiveness of the great God than Whom there is no other deity, the Eternal, the Everlasting, the Living One: I turn to Him for repentance, and beg His grace and forgiveness." This, or a similar form of repentance, is repeated several times. The Muríd then repeats after the Murshid:—"I beg for the favour of God and of the Prophet, and I take for my guide to God (here naming the Murshid) not to change or to separate. God is our witness. By the great God. There is no deity but God. Amín." The Murshid and the Muríd then recite the first chapter of the Qurán, and the Muríd concludes the ceremony by kissing the Murshid's hand.

After the initiatory rite, the Muríd undergoes a series of instructions, including the *Zikrs*, which he is required to repeat daily. The Muríd frequently visits his Murshid, and sometimes the Murshids proceed on a circuit of visitation to their disciples. The place where these "holy men" sit down to instruct the people is ever afterwards held sacred, a small flag is hoisted on a tree, and it is fenced in. Such places are called "*Takiya*," and are protected and kept free from pollution by some Faqír engaged for the purpose.

Those Faqírs who attain to a high degree of sanctity are called *Walís*, the highest rank of which is that of a *Ghaus*. Of such is the Akhund of Swát, on the north-west frontier of India. This celebrated religious leader at the age of eighteen became a member of the Qádiría order of Faqírs; and shortly after his incorporation, he settled down on a small island in the river Indus near Attock, where he lived the life of a recluse for twelve years. During this time, it is said, his only diet was the wild-grass seed and buffalo's milk. He soon acquired a reputation for sanctity, and has gradually become the great religious leader of Central

Asia. He now resides at the village of Seydu in Swát, where he entertains as many as a thousand visitors daily; men from all parts of the Muslim world, who come to hear his wisdom and receive the benefit of his prayers. The Akhund has always been a great opponent of Wahhábí doctrines; and, although he is not well-read in Muslim divinity, his *fatwás* on religious ceremonies and secular observances are received and obeyed by all the Sunní Muhammadans of the north-west frontier of British India.*

---

* An account of the Muhammadan darweshes has been written by Mr. J. P. Brown, Secretary of the United States Legation at Constantinople. Trübner & Co., London.

LI.—ZIKR, OR THE RELIGIOUS SERVICES OF THE DARWESHES.

※Zikr is the religious ceremony, or act of devotion, which is practised by the various religious orders of Faqírs, or Darweshes.※ Almost every religious Muhammadan is a member of some order of Faqírs, and, consequently, the performance of *zikr* is very common in all Muhammadan countries; but it does not appear that any one method of performing the religious service of *zikr*, is peculiar to any particular order.

Zikrs, are of two kinds, *zikr-i-jalí*, that which is recited aloud, and *zikr-i-khafí*, that which is performed either with a low voice, or mentally.

The Naqshbandía order of Faqírs usually perform the latter, whilst the Chishtía and Qádiría orders celebrate the former. There are various ways of going through the exercise, but the main features of each are similar in character. The following is a *zikr-i-jalí* as given in the book Qual-ul-Jamíl, by Maulaví Sháh Walí Ullah, of Delhi :—

1. The worshipper sits in the usual sitting posture and shouts the word *Al-lah* (God), drawing his voice from his left side and then from his throat.

2. Sitting as at prayers he repeats the word *Al-lah* still louder than before, first from his right knee, and then from his left side.

3. Folding his legs under him he repeats the word *Al-lah* first from his right knee and then from his left side, still louder !

4. Still remaining in the same position, he shouts the word *Al-lah*, first from the left knee then from the right knee, then from the left side, and lastly in front, still louder !

5. Sitting as at prayer, with his face towards Mecca, he closes his eyes, says " *Lá* "—drawing the sound as from his navel up to his left shoulder; then he says *i-lá-ha*, drawing out the sound as from his brain; and lastly "*il-lal-lá-ho*," repeated from his left side with great energy.

Each of these stages is called a *Zarb*. They

are, of course, recited many hundreds of times over, and the changes we have described account for the variations of sound and motion of the body described by Eastern travellers who have witnessed the performance of a *zikr*.

The following is a *zikr-i-khafí*, or that which is performed in either a low voice, or mentally.

1. Closing his eyes and lips, he says, " with the tongue of the heart,"

Al-la-ho-sami'un, " God the hearer."

Al-la-ho-baswírun, " God the seer."

Al-la-ho-'alimun, " God the knower."

The first being drawn, as it were, from the navel to the breast; the second, from the breast to the brain; the third, from the brain up to the heavens; and then again repeated stage by stage backwards and forwards.

2. He says in a low voice, "*Allah*," from the right knee, and then from the left side.

3. With each exhalation of his breath, he says, "*lá-iláha*," and with each inhalation, "*il-lal-lá-ho*."

This third *zarb* is a most exhausting act of devotion, performed, as it is, hundreds or even thousands of times, and is, therefore, considered the most meritorious.

It is related that Maulaví Habíb Ullah, now living in the village of Gabásanri, in the Gadún country, on the Peshawur frontier, has become such an adept in the performance of this *zarb*, that he recites the first part of the *zikr-lá-iláha* with the exhalation of his breath after the midday prayer; and the second part, *il-lal-lá-ho*, with the inhalation of his breath before the next time of prayer, thus sustaining his breath for the period of about three hours!

Another act of devotion, which usually accompanies the *zikr*, is that of *Muráqaba*, or meditation.

The worshipper first performs *zikr* of the following:—

Allaho-házarí, " God the present one."
Allaho-názarí, " God the seer."
Allaho-sháhidí, " God who witnesses."
Allaho-maí, " God who is with us."

Having recited this *zikr*, either aloud or mentally, the worshipper proceeds to meditate upon some verse or verses of the Qurán. Those recommended for the Qádiría Faqírs by Maulaví

Sháb Walí Ullah are the following, which we give as indicating the line of thought which is considered most devotional and spiritual by Muslim mystics :—

1. Surat-ul-Hadíd (lvii.), 3.

"He (God) is first. He is last. The Manifest, and the Hidden, and who knoweth all things."

2. Surat-ul-Hadíd (lvii.), 4.

"He (God) is with you wheresoever ye be."

3. Surat-ul-Qáf (l.), 16.

"We (God) are closer to him (man) than his neck vein."

4. Surat-ul-Baqr (ii.), 109.

" Whichever way ye turn, there is the face of God."

5. Surat-un-Nisá (iv.), 125.

" God encompasseth all things."

6. Surat-ur-Rahman (lv.), 7.

" All on earth shall pass away, but the face of thy God shall abide resplendent with majesty and glory."

Some teachers tell their disciples that the heart has two doors, that which is fleshly, and that which is spiritual; and that the *zikr-i-jalí* has been established for the opening of the former, and *zikr-i-khafí* for the latter, in order that they may both be enlightened.

There certainly must be something invigorating in the exercise of a *zikr-i-jalí* to a religious devotee, who seldom stirs out of his mosque; and we have often been told by Maulavís, that they find the performance of a *zikr* keeps evil thoughts from the mind; but as some of the most devoted *zákirs* (*i. e.* those who perform the *zikr*) are amongst the most immoral men, the religious exercise does not appear to have any lasting effect on the moral character.

As a curious instance of the superstitious character of this devotional exercise, the Chishtía order believe that if a man sits cross-legged and seizes the vein called *Kaimús*, which is under the leg, with his toes, that it will give peace to his heart, when accompanied by a *zikr* of the "*nafí isbát*," which is a term used for the first part of the Kalimah, which forms the usual *zikr*, namely :—

Lá-iláha-il-lal-laho, " There is no deity but God."

The most common form of *zikr* is a recital of the ninety-nine names of God; for Muhammad promised those of his followers who recited them, a sure entrance to Paradise.*

---

* *Vide* Mishkát, bk. cxi.

To facilitate this repetition, the *zákir* uses a *Tasbih*, or rosary, of ninety-nine beads. The Wahhábís, however, do not use this invention, but count on their fingers. The introduction of the rosary amongst Roman Catholics is generally ascribed to Dominic, the founder of the Black Friars (A.D. 1221); but Dean Hook says it was in use in the year 1100; it is, therefore, not improbable that the Crusaders borrowed it from their Muslim opponents; and it is thought that the Muhammadans received it from the Buddhists.

There are several lists of the supposed ninety-nine names * of God; but the following is given by Muslim and Bokhárí in their collections of traditions:—

1. Rahmán . . The Compassionate.
2. Rahím . . . The Merciful.
3. Málik . . . The King.
4. Quddus . . The Holy One.
5. Salám . . . The Peace.
6. Momin . . . The Faithful.
7. Mohymin . . The Protector.

---

* Surat-al-Aráf (vii.), 179: "Most excellent titles hath God by these, call ye upon him."

8. 'Azíz	. .	The Incomparable.
9. Jabbár	. .	The Benefactor.
10. Mutakabbir	.	The Mighty Doer.
11. Kháliq	. .	The Creator.
12. Bárí	. .	The Maker.
13. Musawwir	.	The Former.
14. Ghafár	. .	The Pardoner.
15. Qahhár	. .	The Powerful.
16. Wahháb	.	The Giver.
17. Razzáq	. .	The Bestower of Daily Bread.
18. Fattah	. .	The Opener.
19. 'Alím	. .	The Omniscient.
20. Qábiz	. .	The Restrainer.
21. Básit	. .	The Expander.
22. Kháfiz	. .	The Depresser.
23. Ráfí	. .	The Exalter.
24. Mu'iz	. .	The Strengthener.
25. Muzil	. .	The Lowerer.
26. Sami'	. .	The Hearer.
27. Basír	. .	The Seer.
28. Hákam	. .	The Judge.
29. 'Adl	. .	The Just.
30. Latíf	. .	The Benignant.
31. Khabír	. .	The Knower.
32. Halím	. .	The Clement.

33. 'Azím	. .	The Great.
34. Ghafúr	. .	The Great Pardoner.
35. Shakúr	. .	The Rewarder.
36. 'Alí	. .	The Most High.
37. Kabír	. .	The Great Lord.
38. Háfiz	. .	The Guardian.
39. Muqít	. .	The Giver of Strength.
40. Hasíb	. .	The Reckoner.
41. Jalíl	. .	The Glorious.
42. Karím	. .	The Munificent.
43. Raqíb	. .	The Watcher.
44. Mujíb	. .	The Approver of Supplications.
45. Wási'	. .	The Expander.
46. Hakím	. .	The Physician.
47. Wadúd	. .	The All-Loving.
48. Majíd	. .	The Glorious.
49. Báis	. .	The Awakener.
50. Shahíd	. .	The Witness.
51. Haqq	. .	The True.
52. Wakíl	. .	The Provider.
53. Qawwí	. .	The Powerful.
54. Matín	. .	The Firm.
55. Walí	. .	The Friend.
56. Hamíd	. .	The One to be Praised.

57. Muhsí . . . The Counter.
58. Mubdí . . . The Cause.
59. Mu'íd . . . The Restorer.
60. Mohyí . . . The Life-giver.
61. Mumit . . . The Death-giver.
62. Hai . . . The Living.
63. Qaiyyúm . . The Self-subsisting.
64. Wájid . . . The Finder.
65. Majíd . . . The Grand.
66. Wáhid . . . The Unique.
67. Samad . . . The Perpetual.
68. Qádir . . . The Powerful.
69. Muqtadir . . The Prevailing.
70. Muqaddim . . The Bringer before.
71. Muwakhkhir . . The Bringer after.
72. Awwal . . . The First.
73. Akhir . . . The Last.
74. Zahir . . . The Evident.
75. Bátin . . . The Hidden.
76. Wálí . . . The Governor.
77. Muta'á . . . The Sublime.
78. Barr . . . The Doer of Good.
79. Tawwáb . . The Propitious.
80. Muntaqim . . The Avenger.
81. Afú . . . The Eraser.
82. Ráuf . . . The Benefiter.

83.	Málik-ul-Mulk	The King of Kingdoms.
84.	Żuljalál-wal-Ikrám	The Lord of Glory and Honour.
85.	Muksit . . .	The Equitable.
86.	Jámi' . . .	The Assembler.
87.	Ghaní . . .	The Rich.
88.	Mughaní . .	The Enricher.
89.	Mutí . . .	The Giver.
90.	Máni' . . .	The Withholder.
91.	Zárr . . .	The Afflicter.
92.	Náfi' . . .	The Benefactor.
93.	Núr . . .	The Light.
94.	Hádí . . .	The Guide.
95.	Badia' . . .	The Incomparable.
96.	Báqí . . .	The Eternal.
97.	Wáris . . .	The Inheritor.
98.	Rashíd . . .	The Director.
99.	Sabúr . . .	The Patient.

The list either begins or closes with the peculiar designation of God, *Allah*, making the complete number of one hundred names for the Deity.

The following names occur in other works which we have consulted, and are sometimes used in place of some of those in the list already given:—*Azalí*, the Eternal; *Abadí*, the Everlasting; *Maula*, the Lord; *Ahad*, the only One; *Mun'em*, the Giver of Blessing; *Sádiq*, the Righteous One; *Sattár*, the Concealer of Sins; *Rabb*, the Lord.

In the recital of these words the prefix and inflexion are used thus, Ar-Rahímo! Al-Máliko! As-Sami'o! etc. Many of the titles will appear to the English reader to be synonymous, but Muslim theologians discover in them shades of difference. It will be observed that the titles are not arranged in philosophical order.

In addition to the forms of *zikr* already mentioned there are four others which are even of more common use, and are known as *Tasbíh*, *Tahmíd*, *Tahlíl*, and *Takbír*. They are used as exclamations of joy and surprise, as well as for the devotional exercise of *zikr*.

Tasbíh is the expression *Subhán-Allah!* "Holiness be to God!"

Tahmíd. *Alhamdo-Lilla!* "Praise be to God!"

Tahlíl. *Lá-il-la-ha-il-lal-lá-ho!* "There is no deity but God!"

Takbír. *Allaho-Akbar!* "God is great!"

Muhammad said, "Repeat the Tasbíh a hundred times, and a thousand virtues shall be recorded by God for you, ten virtuous deeds for each repetition."

When the *Tasbíh* and *Tahmíd* are recited together it is said thus, *Subhán-Allah wa Bihamdihi*, *i. e.*, "Holiness be to God with His praise." It is related in the Hadís that Muhammad said, "Whoever recites this sentence a hundred times, morning and evening, will have all his sins forgiven."

In forming our estimation of Muhammad and Muhammadanism we must take into consideration the important place the devotional exercise of *zikr* occupies in the system, not forgetting that it has had the authoritative sanction of " the Prophet " himself.

LII.—THE LORD JESUS CHRIST.

IN the Qurán our blessed Lord is spoken of as '*Isa* (Jesus), and *Masíh* (the Messiah). He is also called *Kalima*,* the Word (of God); *Qaul-ul-Haqq*,† the Word of Truth ; and *Rúh*, the Spirit (of God); *Rúh-Ullah*, the Spirit of God, being the special title, or *Kalima*, whereby Jesus is distinguished from the other great prophets. He is one "illustrious in this world and in the next," and "who has near access to God."‡ He is "*God's Apostle* to confirm the law, and to announce an apostle that should come after, whose name shall be

---

* Surat-un-Nisá (iv.), 169.

† Surat-ul-Maryam (xix.), 35. The passage is translated by Rodwell, as well as by Persian commentators, "this is a statement of the truth"; but according to Bezáwí, the words *Qaul-ul-Haqq* may be taken as a title of Jesus Christ, *i. e.* the Word of Truth.

‡ Surat-i-Ál-i-'Imrán (iii.), 40.

Ahmad."* He is said to have been born of Mary, the sister of Aaron, and the daughter of 'Imrán, near the trunk of a palm tree; to have spoken in his cradle, and to have performed many miracles during his infancy; to have cured the blind and the leper; to have chosen apostles, and to have caused a table to descend from heaven, both as "a festival and a sign for them." The Jews are said to have been deceived by God, and to have crucified another person instead of Jesus, who was taken up into heaven, where he remains with his mother in a lofty and quiet place, watered with springs, until he shall come again in the last day to convert the whole world to Islám!

The rambling incoherent account of our blessed Lord's life, as given in the Qurán, would far exceed the limits of these "Notes"; but it will be found upon reference to the following Súras, or chapters:—

An account of the birth of the Virgin Mary.—Súra iii. 33–37, 42–44.

Birth of Jesus announced to the Virgin Mary.—Súra iii. 45–48; xix. 16–21.

---

* Surat-us-Sáf (lxi.), 6.

The birth of Jesus.—Súra xix. 22–28.

The miracles of the Infancy.—Súra xix. 29–32; iii. 48; v. 119.

His prophetical mission.—Súra v. 87; xxxiii. 7; xliii. 56–63; lxi. 6.

His choice of apostles.—Súra iii. 51–52; lxi. 14.

The Lord's table.—Súra v. 121–124.

His crucifixion.—Súra iii. 53–54; iv. 156–158; v. 119; xix. 32; iii. 54.

His assumption with the Virgin Mary into Paradise.—Súra xxiii. 52.

His second Advent.—Súra xliii. 59.

He must render an account of himself to God.—Súra xxiii. 7, 8; v. 118–119, 125, 127; iv. 158.

There is a remarkable Hadís related by Anas, which inadvertently proves that, whilst Muhammad admitted his own sinfulness, as well as that of other prophets, he could not charge our Lord with sin. It is as follows:—" The Prophet of God said, ' In the day of resurrection Musalmáns will not be able to move, and they will be greatly distressed, and will say, " Would to God that we had asked Him to create some-one to intercede for us, that we might be taken from this place, and be delivered from tribulation and sorrow?" Then these men will go to Adam, and will say, "Thou art the father of all men, God created thee with His hand, and made thee a dweller in Paradise, and ordered His angels to prostrate themselves before thee, and taught thee the names of all things. Ask grace for us we pray thee!" And Adam will say, "I am not of that degree of eminence you suppose, for I committed a sin in eating of the tree which was forbidden. Go to Noah, the Prophet, he was the first who was sent by God to the unbelievers on the face of the earth." Then they will go to Noah and ask for intercession, and he will say, "I am not of that degree which ye suppose." And he will remember the sin which he committed in asking the Lord for the deliverance of his son (Hud), not knowing whether it was a right request or not; and he will say, " Go to Abraham, who is the Friend of God." Then they will go to Abraham, and he will say, "I am not of that degree which ye suppose." And he will remember the three occasions upon which he told lies in the world; and he will say, "Go to Moses, who is the servant to whom God gave

His law, and whom He allowed to converse with Him." And they will go to Moses, and Moses will say, "I am not of that degree which ye suppose." And he will remember the sin which he committed in slaying a man, and he will say, "Go to Jesus, He is the servant of God, the Apostle of God, the Spirit of God, and the Word of God." Then they will go to Jesus, and He will say, "Go to Muhammad who is a servant, whose sins God has forgiven both first and last." Then the Musalmáns will come to me, and I will ask permission to go into God's presence and intercede for them.'" (*Vide* Mishkát, bk. xxiii. chap. xii.)

LIII.—THE CRUCIFIXION OF OUR SAVIOUR.

THE following are the verses in the Qurán which allude to our blessed Lord's crucifixion:
Surat-un-Nisá (iv.), 157:—
" And for their saying (*we have cursed them*), ' Verily we have slain the Messiah, Jesus the son of Mary, and Apostle of God.' Yet they slew him not, and they crucified him not; but they had only his likeness. And they who differed about him were in doubt concerning him; no sure knowledge had they about him, but followed only an opinion, and they did not really slay him, but God took him up to Himself."
Surat-ul-Maida (v.), 19:—
" They are infidels who say, ' Verily God is the Messiah, the son of Mary.' Say: And who could obtain anything from God to the contrary if he chose to destroy the Messiah, the

son of Mary, and his mother, and the whole world also."

Surat-i-A'l-i-Imrán (iii.), 47, 48 :—

" The Jews plotted and God plotted : but of those who plot is God the best. Remember when God said, 'O Jesus! verily I will cause thee to die, and will take thee up to myself and deliver thee from those who believe not; and I will place those who follow thee above those who believe not until the day of resurrection. Then to me is your return, and wherein ye differ will I decide between you.' "

Whilst all Muslim commentators are agreed as to the literal interpretation of these passages, there is some difference as to the person crucified in Christ's stead.

1. In the Tafsír-i-Bezáwí it is said that Christ asked one of his disciples to take his place.

2. In the Tafsír-i-Mazhárí, that God took Christ in his human body to heaven alive.

3. In the Tafsír-i-Baghwí, that God transformed Christ's appearance to one of his enemies, a spy, who was thus crucified in his stead by mistake.

4. In the Tafsír-i-Kalbí, that *Titánús* was

crucified, God having transferred Christ's appearance to that person.

5. In the Tafsír-i-Kamálain that Christ was dead seven hours, then restored to life and taken to heaven.

It will be seen that these commentators have adopted the errors of the Basilidians, and other heretics, with reference to our Lord's crucifixion; for Irenæus says that the Basilidians held that Simon of Cyrene was crucified instead of Christ.

The "Cross of Christ" is the missing link in the Muslim's creed; for we have already alluded to the great anomaly of a religion which rejects the doctrine of a sacrifice for sin, whilst its great central feast is *a Feast of Sacrifice*.

It is related by the Muslim historian Waqidi, that Muhammad had such repugnance to the sign of the cross, that he destroyed everything brought to his house with that figure upon it.

LIV.—THE DIVINITY OF CHRIST, AND THE HOLY TRINITY.

The following are the allusions to the Holy Trinity and the Sonship of Christ in the Qurán:—

Surat-un-Nisá (iv.), 169:—

"O ye people of the Book! overstep not bounds in your religion, and of God speak only truth. The Messiah Jesus, son of Mary, is only an Apostle of God, and his Word which he conveyed into Mary, and a Spirit proceeding from himself. Believe, therefore, in God and his apostles, and say not there is a Trinity (lit. "three"). Forbear, it will be better for you. God is only one God! Far be it from His glory that He should have a son * * * * The Messiah disdaineth not to be a servant of God."

Surat-ul-Maida (v.), 79:—

"The Messiah, the son of Mary, is but an

apostle; other apostles have flourished before him, and his mother was a just person; they both ate food."

Verse 116 of the same Súra:—

"O Jesus, son of Mary, hast thou said unto mankind, 'Take me and my mother as two Gods beside God?'"

From the above verses it appears that Muhammad thought the Holy Trinity of the Christians consisted of the Father, the Son, and the Virgin; and historians tell us that there existed in Arabia a sect called Collyridians, who considered the Virgin Mary a divine person, and offered in worship to her a cake called Collyris; it is, therefore, not improbable that Muhammad obtained his perverted notion of the Holy Trinity from the existence of this sect. From the expression "they both ate food," we must conclude that Muhammad had but a sensuous idea of the Trinity in Unity, and had never been instructed in the orthodox faith with reference to this dogma.

In dealing with Muhammadans the Christian missionary must not treat their system as though the views of Islám were precisely those of modern Socinians.* Islám admits the miraculous conception of Christ, and that he is the "*Word*" which God "conveyed into Mary;" and whilst the other five great prophets are but "the chosen," "the preacher," "the friend," "the converser with," and "the messenger" of God, Jesus is admitted to be the "*Spirit of God.*" He is the greatest miracle worker of all the prophets, and whilst Muhammad is dead and buried, and saw corruption, all Muslim divines admit that Jesus "saw no corruption," and still lives with a human body in Paradise.

Moreover, it is said in the Hadís that the *Núr-i-Muhammad*, the light of Muhammad, was created before all things which were made by God. The pre-existence of the divine "Word which was made flesh and dwelt amongst us" is not, therefore, an idea foreign to the Muslim mind.

---

* We speak of the views of *modern* Socinians, for we are aware that both the Socini, uncle and nephew, admitted the miraculous conception of Christ, and said that He ought to be worshipped.

LV. — TAHRI'F, OR THE ALLEGED CORRUPTION OF THE SACRED BOOKS BY THE JEWS AND CHRISTIANS.

TAHRI'F is the word used by Muhammadan writers to express the corruption of the sacred Scriptures of the Jews and Christians, as asserted in the Qurán.

Imám Fakhar-ud-dín Rází, in his commentary, explains "*Tahríf*" to mean, to change, alter, or turn aside anything from the truth. Muslim divines say there are two kinds of *Tahríf*, namely, *Tahríf-i-M'anawí*, a corruption of the meaning; and *Tahríf-i-Lafzí*, a corruption of the words.

Muhammadan controversialists, when they become acquainted with the nature of the contents of our sacred books, and of the impossibility of reconciling the contents of the Qurán with those of the sacred Scriptures, charge the Christians with the *Tahríf-i-Lafzí*. They say the Christians have expunged the word *Ahmad* from the prophecies, and have inserted the expression "Son of God," and the story of the crucifixion, death, and resurrection of our blessed Lord. This view, however, is not the one held by the most celebrated of the Muslim commentators.

Imám Muhammad Ismaíl Bokhárí,* records that Ibn 'Abbás said that "the word *Tahríf* (corruption) signifies to change a thing from its original nature; and that there is no man who could corrupt a single word of what proceeded from God, so that the Jews and Christians could corrupt only by misrepresenting the *meaning* of the words of God."

Ibn-i-Mazar and Ibn Abi Hátim state, in the commentary known as the Tafsír Durr-i-Mansúr, that they have it on the authority of Ibn-i-Munía, that the *Taurát* (*i. e.* the books of Moses), and the *Injíl* (*i. e.* the Gospels), are in the same state of purity in which they were

---

* *Vide* Hadís-i-Sahíh-Bokhárí, edition printed at the Matba' Ahmadi Meerut, A.H. 1284 (A.D. 1867), p. 1127, line 7.

sent down from heaven, and that no alterations had been made in them, but that the Jews were wont to deceive the people by unsound arguments, and by wresting the sense of Scripture.

Sháh Walí Ullah, in his commentary, the *Fauz-ul-Kabír*, and also Ibn 'Abbás, support the same view.

This appears to be the correct interpretation of the various verses of the Qurán charging the Jews with having corrupted the meaning of the sacred Scriptures.

For example, Surat-i-A'l-i-Imrám (iii.), 78: " There are certainly some of them who read the Scriptures perversely, that ye may think what they read to be really in the Scriptures, yet it is not in the Scriptures; and they say this is from God, but it is not from God; and they speak that which is false concerning God against their own knowledge."

Imám Fakhar-ud-dín, in his commentary on this verse, and many others of the same character which occur in the Qurán, says it refers to a *Tahríf-i-M'anawí*, and that it does not mean that the Jews altered the text, but merely that they made alterations in the course of reading.

But whilst all the old commentators, who most probaby had never seen a copy of the sacred Books of the Jews and Christians, only charge us with a *Tahríf-i-M'anawí*, all modern controversialists amongst the Muhammadans contend for a *Tahríf-i-Lafzí*, as being the only solution of the difficulty.

In dealing with such opponents, the Christian divine will avail himself of the following arguments :—

1. The Qurán does not charge the Jews and Christians with corrupting the text of their sacred books; and all the learned Muslim commentators admit that such is not the case.

2. The Qurán asserts that the Holy Scriptures of the Jews and Christians existed in the days of Muhammad, who invariably speaks of them with reverence and respect.

3. There now exist manuscripts of the Old and New Testaments of an earlier date than that of Muhammad (A.D. 610–632).

4. There are versions of the Old and New Testament now extant, which existed before

Muhammad; for example, the Septuagint, the Latin Vulgate, the Syriac, the Coptic, and the Armenian versions.

5. The Hexapla, or Octapla of Origen, which dates four centuries before Muhammad, gives various versions of the Old Testament Scriptures in parallel columns.

6. The Syrian Christians of St. Thomas,* of Malabar and Travancore, in the south of India, who were separated from the western world for centuries, possess the same Scriptures.

7. In the works of Justin Martyr, who lived from A.D. 103 to 167, there are numerous quotations from our sacred books, which prove that they were exactly the same as those we have now. The same may be said of other early Christian writers.

Muhammadan controversialists of the present day urge that the numerous readings which exist in the Christian books are a proof that they have been corrupted. But these do not

---

* That Christians existed in India at a very early period is plain from the fact that a Bishop of India signed his name at the Council of Nice, A.D. 325.

affect, in the least, the main points at issue between the Christian and the Muslim. The Divine Sonship of Christ, the Fatherhood of God, the Crucifixion, Death, and Resurrection of Christ, and the Atonement, are all clearly stated in almost every book of the New Testament, whilst they are rejected by the Qurán.

The most plausible of modern objections urged by Muslim divines is, that the Christians have *lost* the *Injíl* which was sent down from heaven to Jesus; and that the New Testament contains merely the *Hadís*, or *Sunna*—the *traditions* handed down by Matthew, Mark, Luke, John, Paul, and others. It is, of course, a mere assertion, unsupported by any proof; but it appears to be a line of argument which commends itself to Sayyid Ahmad Khán, C.S.I.,[*] and also to Ameer 'Alí Maulaví, M.A., LL.B.[†] The latter professes to be a Muhammadan

---

[*] *Vide* The Muhammadan Commentaries on the Holy Bible, Part I., by Syud Ahmad Khan, C.S.I. Ghazeepore, 1862.

[†] *Vide* The Life and Teachings of Muhammad, by Syud Ameer Ali Moulvie, M.A., LL.B., of the Inner Temple, Barrister-at-Law. London, 1873.

rationalist; but as Islám is a system of the most positive *dogma*, it does not admit either of rationalism, or "free thought." Sayyid Ahmad and Ameer 'Alí no more represent the Muhammadanism of the Qurán and the Traditions, than the opinions of Mr. Voysey represent the teaching of orthodox Christianity.

"Islámism is in itself stationary, and was framed thus to remain; sterile, like its God, lifeless like its first principle in all that constitutes life—for life is love, participation, and progress, and of these the Coranic deity has none. It justly repudiates all change, all development. To borrow the forcible words of Lord Houghton, the written book is there the dead man's hand, stiff and motionless; whatever savours of vitality is by that alone convicted of heresy and defection." *

---

* Palgrave's Arabia, vol. i. p. 372.

INDEX

OF

TECHNICAL TERMS.

A.

'Abid, 158.
Abu-Dáúd, 56.
Ahádís, 12.
Ahl-i-Kitáb, 11.
Akhiri Chahár Shambah, 167.
Alfáz, 31.
'Alim, 157.
Al-kitáb, 15.
Allah, 67.
'Amm, 31, 64.
Ansár, 24, 62.
'Aqáid, 161.
Arb'áa-ul-Akhír, 167.
'Asar, 114.
Asháb, 62.
'Ashiq, 229.
'Ashúrá'a, 163.
'Ashúr-Khána, 164.

Attahíyat, 110.
'Aúzobillah, 107.
Ayat, 28.
Ayyám-ul-Tashríq, 135.
Azád, 234.
Azán, 105, 116.
Azráíl, 79.

B.

Bahisht, 91.
Bait-Ullah, 133.
Baqr-i-'Id, 173.
Bára-Wafát, 168.
Ba Shara', 234.
Be`Shara', 234.
Bint-i-Labún, 126.
Bint-i-Mukház, 126.
Bokhárí, 58.

C.

Chást, 114.
Chishtía, 236.

D.

Dábbat-ul-Arz, 88.
Dajjál, 88.
Dalálat, 35.
Darúd, 111.
Dár-ul-Harb, 207.
Dár-ul-Islám, 207.
Dár-ul-Qarár, 92.
Dár-us-Salám, 91.
Darwesh, 234.
Díat, 142.
Dígar, 114.
Dín, 11.
Dirham, 127.
Dozakh, 96.
Dua', 32, 111.

F.

Faná, 229.
Faqíh, 157.
Faqír, 158, 234.
Farz, 112, 137.
Farz-i-Kafáí, 146.
Fátihah, 107.
Fatwá, 144, 156.
Firdaus, 91.
Fiqah, 161.
Fitrat, 147.
Fúrqán, 14.

G.

Ghaus, 158, 241.
Ghází, 206.
Ghusal, 105.
Gísú, 230.

H.

Hadd, 141.
Hadís, 50, 160.
Hadís-i-'Azíz, 54.
Hadís-i-Gharíb, 54.
Hadís-i-Hasan, 52.
Hadís-i-Maqtu', 53.
Hadís-i-Marfu', 52.
Hadís-i-Mashhúr, 54, 62.
Hadís-i-Mauqúf, 53.
Hadís-i-Mauzu', 55.
Hadís-i-Mursal, 54.
Hadís-i-Mustafíz, 54.
Hadís-i-Mutawátir, 53, 62.
Hadís-i-Sahíh, 52.
Hadís-i-Z'aíf, 52.
Hájí, 135.
Hajj, 101, 130.
Hajr-ul-Aswad, 133.
Hakím, 157.
Halál, 143.
Hambali, 213.
Hanifí, 212.
Haqíqat, 34, 229, 230.
Haqíqí, 226.
Harám, 138.
Harf, 28.
Hashíyah, 162.

Háwía, 97.
Hijrat, 2, 209.
Hiqqah, 126.
Hutama, 96.

I.

'Ibárat, 32, 35.
Iblís, 32, 82.
Ibn-i-Májah, 56.
'Idgah, 171.
'Id-ul-Azhá, 134, 173.
'Id-ul-Fitr, 128, 171.
'Ifrít, 82.
Ihrám, 132.
I'jáb, 177.
'Ijma', 12, 61.
Ilhám, 47, 48.
Ilhám Rabbání, 47.
Illat, 64.
'Ilm-i-Hadís, 51.
'Ilm-i-Tajwíd, 25.
'Ilm-i-Usúl, 31.
Imám, 150, 156.
Imám-Bára, 164.
Imám-Mahdí, 89.
Imám-ul-'Azam, 150.
Imám-ul-Mubín, 98.
I'mán, 66.
I'mán-i-Mufassal, 66.
I'mán-i-Mujmal, 66.
Injíl, 268.
Iqámat, 106, 117.
Iqtizá, 35.
'Isa, 256.
'Ishaq, 228.
Ishárat, 35.
Ishárat-ul-Malak, 48.

Islám, 10.
Ism-i-Safát, 67.
Ism-i-Zát, 67.
Ism-ul-'Azam, 67.
Istibsár, 57.
Istidlál, 35.
Istighfár, 179.
Isti'mál, 34.
Isráfíl, 79.
Itifáq-i-F"ili, 61.
Itifáq-i-Qauli, 61.
Itifáq-i-Saqúti, 61.
'Itiqáf, 121.
Izn, 225.

J.

Jabarút, 230.
Jahannam, 96.
Jahím, 97.
Jalálíá, 236.
Jamád-ul-úla, 163.
Jamád-ul-ukhrá, 163.
Jama'-i-Masjid, 171.
Jamra, 134.
Janáza, 185.
Jánn, 82.
Jannat, 91.
Jannat-i-'Adan, 92.
Jannat-i-'Illiyún, 92.
Jannat-ul-Firdaus, 92.
Jannat-ul-Khuld, 91.
Jannat-ul-Mawá, 92.
Jannat-un-N'aím, 92.
Jaz'ah, 126.
Jibráíl, 15, 79.

Jihád, 206.
Jihád-ul-Akbar, 206.
Jihád-ul-Asghar, 206.
Jinn, 82.
Jizíyah, 209.
Juz, 30.

K.

K'aba, 131.
Kabíra, 136, 139.
Káfi, 57.
Kalimah, 28, 102, 179, 256.
Kalám-Ullah, 12, 15.
Kalím-Ullah, 84.
Karína, 32.
Khabar-i-Wáhid, 54, 62.
Khafí, 32, 33, 37.
Khalífa, 150.
Khalíl-Ullah, 85.
Khán, 159.
Kháss, 31, 64.
Khatíb, 198.
Khatnah, 103.
Khudá, 68.
Khusús-ul-'ain, 31.
Khusús-ul-jins, 31.
Khusús-ul-nau', 31.
Khutbah, 134, 198.
Kináyah, 35.
Kitáb, 15, 85.
Kitábíah, 217.
Kirám-ul-Katibím, 80.
Kufr, 37, 139.

L.

Láhd, 191, 192.
Láhút, 230.
Lahw-ul-Mahfúz, 98.
Laylut-ul-Mubarak, 123, 169.
Laylut-ul-Qadr, 121.
Lazwá, 96.

M.

Madarris, 157.
Mahr, 179.
Mai-khána, 230.
Majáz, 34.
Majází, 226.
Majúj, 88.
Majusí, 217.
Majzúb, 234.
Makrúh, 138.
Malak, 16, 79.
Malakút, 230.
Malang, 237.
Málik, 80.
Málikí, 207, 213.
Man - lá - yastahzirah - al - faqíh, 57.
Mansúkh, 38.
Mantiq, 162.
Manzil, 30, 228.
Maqám-i-Ibrahím, 133.
Márid, 82.
M'arifat, 229, 230.
M'ashuq, 230.
Masíh, 256.

Masíh-ul-Dajjál, 88.
Masjid-ul-Harám, 133.
Mátam, 163.
Matan, 162.
Maulaví, 157, 238.
Maulúd, 226.
Mazhab, 11.
Mihráb, 203.
Mikáíl, 79.
Millat, 11.
Mimbar, 171, 198.
Míqát, 132.
Mír, 159.
Misqál, 127.
Miswák, 147.
Mitraqat, 80.
Miyán, 159.
Mízán, 89.
Momin, 11.
Mua'qqibát, 80.
Muawattáa, 57.
Muawwal, 32.
Muazzin, 116, 198.
Mubáh, 138.
Mudária, 237.
Mufassar, 32.
Mufassir, 157.
Mufsíd, 138.
Muftí, 156.
Muhaddis, 157.
Muhájir, 62, 209.
Muhammad, 1.
Muharram, 163.
Muhaqqiq, 157.
Muhkam, 33.
Mujmal, 33.
Mujtahid, 157.
Mujtahidín, 48, 61.
Mulla, 157.
Munáját, 112, 171.

Munkar, 80.
Munqata', 53.
Muráqaba, 246.
Muríd, 240.
Murshid, 227, 240.
Murtadd, 141.
Musalmán, 11.
Mushkil, 33.
Mushrik, 225.
Mushtarak, 31.
Muslim, 56.
Mustahab, 138.
Mut'ah, 178.
Mutakallim, 157.
Mutashábih, 34.
Muttasil, 53.
Muwahhid, 225.

N.

Nabí, 102.
Nabi-Ullah, 84.
Nafl, 112.
Nafí-isbát, 248.
Nahaj-ul-Balághat, 57.
Nahw, 162.
Nájíah, 232.
Nakír, 80.
Namáz, 32, 104.
Namáz-i-Dígar, 114.
Namáz-i-Khuftan, 114.
Namáz-i-Peshín, 114.
Namáz-i-Shám, 114.
Namáz-i-Subh, 114.
Námús, 18.
Naqshbandía, 235.
Nárawá, 137.
Nasaí, 56.

Nass, 32.
Násikh, 39.
Nasuá, 200.
Násút, 228, 230.
Nazr, 226.
Nikah, 177.
Nisf, 30.
Niyyat, 106.
Nmúz, 104, 114.
Núr-i-Muhammad, 266.

P.

Paighambar, 102.
Peshín, 114.
Pír, 157.

Q.

Qabúl, 177.
Qádaría, 236.
Qaul-ul-Haqq, 256.
Qazá, 120.
Qazaf, 140.
Qází, 155.
Qíám, 106.
Qíám-i-Sami-Ullah, 108.
Qíámat, 87.
Qiús, 12, 48, 64.
Qíás-i-Jalí, 64.
Qíás-i-Khafí, 64.
Qibla, 135.
Qira'at, 24, 107.
Qisás, 142.
Qurbán-Bayrám, 173.
Qurbán-i-'Id, 173.
Qurán, 12, 14.
Qurán-Majíd, 14.

Qurán-Sharíf, 14.
Qutab, 158.
Qutbah, 158.

R.

Rabi'-ul-Awwal, 163.
Rabi'-ul-Akhir, 163.
Rafía, 237.
Rajab, 163.
Rak'at, 110.
Ramazán, 119, 163.
Rami-ul-Jamár, 134.
Rasúl, 84, 102.
Rasúl-Ullah, 85.
Rawá, 137.
Rayyán, 119.
Rezwán, 80.
Riwáyat, 54.
Roza, 101.
Rowzat-us-Shuhádáa, 165.
Ruba', 30.
Rúh, 256.
Rúh-Ullah, 85, 256.
Rúh-ul-Amín, 15.
Rúh-ul-Qudus, 15.
Ruku', 30.

S.

Sab'ata-Ahrúf, 25.
Sadaqa, 128, 171.
Safar, 163.
Saghíra, 139.
Sáhib-i-Nissab, 125.
Sahífah, 85.
S'aír, 97.
Salám, 112, 148.

INDEX.

Sálik, 229, 234.
Saqar, 97.
Sarf, 162.
Saríh, 34.
Sarwardía, 236.
Sayyid, 159.
Sift-ul-Imán, 180.
Siháh-Sittah, 57, 160.
Silsilah, 235.
Sipára, 30.
Sírát, 90.
Síyar, 162.
Sh'abán, 163.
Shab-i-Barát, 123, 169.
Shab-Qadr, 170.
Shádí, 177.
Shadíd-ul-Quá, 15.
Sháfa'í, 207, 212.
Shahíd, 211.
Shaitán, 82.
Sharáb, 230.
Sharh, 162.
Sharíat, 230.
Shawwál, 163.
Shekh, 158.
Shekh-ul-Islám, 155.
Shía'h, 12.
Subhán, 106.
Súfí, 227.
Sufi-Ullah, 84.
Sulát, 101, 104.
Sulát-ul-'Asar, 114.
Sulát-ul-Fajr, 114.
Sulát-ul-'Ishaa, 114.
Sulát-ul-Ishráq, 114.
Sulát-ul-Istikhárah, 116.
Sulát-ul-Juma', 115.
Sulát-ul-Khasúf, 116.
Sulát-ul-Khauf, 116.
Sulát-ul-Kusúf, 116.

Sulát-ul-Maghríb, 114.
Sulát-ul-Musáfir, 115.
Sulát-ut-Tahajúd, 114.
Sulát-ut-Taráwih, 116.
Sulát-uz-Zuha, 114.
Sulát-uz-Zuhr, 114.
Suls, 30.
Sunna, 50.
Sunnat, 112.
Sunnat-i-F"ili, 137.
Sunnat-i-Qaulí, 137.
Sunnat-i-Taqrírí, 137.
Sunní, 12.
Surá, 29.

T.

Tab'aín, 53.
Taba' Tab'aín, 62.
Tabíb, 156.
Tafsír, 161.
Tahlíl, 254.
Tahmíd, 254.
Tahríf, 267.
Tahríf-i-Lafzí, 267.
Tahríf-i-M'anawí, 267.
Tahzíb, 57.
Takbír, 188, 254.
Takbír-i-Jalsa, 109.
Takbír-i-Qa'úd, 110.
Takbír-i-Qíám, 110.
Takbír-i-Ruku', 108.
Takbír-i-Sijdah, 109.
Takbír-i-Tahrímah, 106.
Takía, 217.
Takiya, 238, 241.
Taláq, 182.
Taláq-i-Ahsan, 182.

Taláq-i-Bid'aí, 183.
Taláq-i-Hasan, 182.
Taláq-i-Mutlaq, 183.
Tálib, 228.
Taqdír, 98.
Taráwih, 121.
Taríqat, 230, 234.
Tarwíah, 134.
Tasawwaf, 227.
Tasbíh, 249, 254.
Tasbíh-i-Ruku', 108.
Tasbíh-i-Sijdah, 108, 109.
Tashahhúd, 111.
Tasmíyah, 107.
Taurát, 268.
T'auuz, 107.
Tawáf, 133, 225.
T'azír, 142.
Tirmízí, 56.

U.

'Ubudíyat, 194, 228.
'Ulama, 157.
'Urs, 177.
Usúl, 160.

W.

Wahhábí, 219.
Wáhí, 47.
Wáhí-Bátin, 48.

Wáhí-Ghair-i-Matlu', 60.
Wáhí-Qalb, 48.
Wáhí-Qurán, 47.
Wáhí-Záhir, 47.
Wajd, 229.
Wájib, 137.
Walí, 47, 157, 241.
Wasl, 229.
Witr, 112.
Wuzu, 105.

Y.

Yajúj, 88.
Yaum-un-Nahr, 173.

Z.

Záhid, 158.
Záhir, 32, 47.
Zakát, 101, 125.
Zákir, 248.
Zarb, 244.
Zát, 37.
Zikr, 243.
Zikr-i-Jalí, 243.
Zikr-i-Khafí, 243.
Zimmí, 209.
Zuhd, 229.
Zul-Hijja, 135, 163.
Zul-Q'ada, 163.

London: Printed by W. H. Allen & Co., 13, Waterloo Place, S.W.

Opinions of the Press on the First Edition.

" Altogether an admirable little book. It combines two excellent qualities, abundance of facts and lack of theories . . . On every one of the numerous heads (over fifty) into which the book is divided, Mr. Hughes furnishes a large amount of very valuable information, which it would be exceedingly difficult to collect from even a large library of works on the subject. The book might well be called a 'Dictionary of Muhammadan Theology,' for we know of no English work which combines a methodical arrangement (and consequently facility of reference), with fulness of information in so high a degree as the little volume before us."—*The Academy.* (Review by Mr. Stanley Lane Poole.)

"It contains *multum in parvo*, and is about the best outlines of the tenets of the Muslim faith which we have seen. It has, moreover, the rare merit of being accurate; and, although it contains a few passages which we would gladly see expunged, it cannot fail to be useful to all Government *employés*, who have to deal with Muhammadans; whilst to Missionaries, it will be invaluable."—*The Times of India.* (Review by Colonel W. Nassau Lees, LL.D.)

"This small book is the most luminous, most convenient, and, we think, the most accurate, outline of the tenets and practices of Islamism that we have met with. It seems exactly the sort of comprehensive and trustworthy book, in small compass, on this subject, that we and many more have often looked for in vain. . . . The author has evidently studied his subject in a faithful, laborious, and scholarly manner; and has not only studied, but mastered it. The work is of great value for general students, and for men whose work lies among the Musulman population, such as civil servants, and missionaries, it seems to be the very work that is wanted."—*The Friend of India.*

"It is manifest throughout the work that we have before us the opinions of one thoroughly conversant with the subject, and who is uttering no random notions. . . . We strongly recommend ' *Notes on Muhammadanism.*' Our clergy especially, even though they are not missionaries, and have no intention of labouring amongst Muhammadans, or consorting with them, ought to have at least as much knowledge of the system as can be most readily acquired, with a very little careful study, from this useful treatise."—*The Record.*

"The main object of the work is to reveal the real and practical character of the Islam faith, and in this the author has evidently been successful."—*The Standard.*

"Its value as a means of correcting the common impressions about Islam will reveal itself to the most cursory reader, while the author's evident scholarship and intimate knowledge of his subject, bespeak for him a patient hearing on points the most open to controversy."—*Indian Mail.*

"Mr. Hughes has done good service by providing, in the shape of these 'Notes,' a concise, well arranged, and convenient hand-book of Islam; so small that all missionaries can easily find time to master it, yet so comprehensive that the information it gives will be found sufficient—not, indeed, for the curious investigator of the science, but for the ordinary Indian missionary. . . . Knowledge for which, otherwise, we should be compelled to search through large volumes in many languages, is here brought together in the compass of a small octavo."—*Indian Evangelical Review.*

"In brief compass it contains a large amount of reliable information. Instead of theories and fancies, facts are placed before us. Muhammadanism is represented as it really is, not as it is supposed that it might possibly be. Instead of retailing the speculations current in literary society at home, Mr. Hughes furnishes us with brief but incisive statements, which, so far as they go, leave nothing to be desired."—*The Church Missionary Intelligencer.*

www.ingramcontent.com/pod-product-compliance
Lightning Source LLC
Chambersburg PA
CBHW032046230426
43672CB00009B/1495